Conversations
With Heaven

D1142891

By the same author

An Angel Called My Name
An Angel Healed Me
An Angel Spoke to Me
How to Speak to Your Angels
How to See Your Angels
Celtic Angels
The Afterlife Is Real

Conversations With Heaven

THERESA CHEUNG

**SIMON &
SCHUSTER**

London · New York · Sydney · Toronto · New Delhi

A CBS COMPANY

First published in Great Britain by Simon & Schuster UK Ltd, 2014
A CBS COMPANY

Copyright © 2014 by Theresa Cheung

This book is copyright under the Berne convention.
No reproduction without permission.
All rights reserved.

The right of Theresa Cheung to be identified as the authors of this
work has been asserted by her in accordance with sections 77 and 78
of the Copyright, Designs and Patents Act, 1988.

1 3 5 7 9 10 8 6 4 2

Simon & Schuster UK Ltd
1st Floor
222 Gray's Inn Road
London WC1X 8HB

www.simonandschuster.co.uk

Simon & Schuster Australia
Sydney

A CIP catalogue record for this book is available
from the British Library.

Paperback ISBN: 978-1-47111-238-6
Ebook ISBN: 978-1-47111-239-3

Typeset by Hewer Text UK Ltd, Edinburgh
Printed and Bound in Great Britain by
CPI Group (UK) Ltd, Croydon CR0 4YY

Contents

Acknowledgements

Each time a book about matters spiritual is published it feels like a blessing and a miracle – especially when you consider the harsh and difficult economic times we live in. As always, I am deeply grateful to my fantastic agent, Clare Hulton, and my inspiring editor, Kerri Sharp, for their support, and to everyone at Simon & Schuster involved in the process of making this book happen.

Heartfelt thanks go to all the amazing people who contributed their stories to this book. I want you to know that you are making a real difference to the lives of others by bringing comfort, hope and inspiration. You may not realize it but you are changing and saving lives with your words.

And while we are on the subject of changing lives with words, more heartfelt thanks go to Kate Adams for her wonderful words and helping hands with gathering and editing stories for this book. I literally could not have completed it without you – thank you. Kate's website is www.selfhelpcentral.co.uk and you will see how working on this book brought back a few memories for her and also how something new and fascinating happened to her right in the middle of the editing process.

That's death and life, you see. We all shine on. You just have to release your hearts, alert your senses, and pay attention. A leaf, a star, a song, a laugh. Notice all the little things, because somebody is reaching out to you. Qualcuno ti ama. *Somebody loves you.*

Ben Sherwood,
The Death and Life of Charlie St Cloud

In the beginning

What happens on earth is only the beginning.
Mitch Albom

I was born into a family of psychics and spiritualists; some of my earliest, brightest memories are of sitting in the back of a room as my great-aunt Rose did her demonstrations. My grandmother and mother also had the gift of sensing and communicating with spirits – it was just the way things were in our family. So it won't come as a shock for you to know that I have a strong belief in the afterlife, that I believe it is possible to talk to departed loved ones. I've written many books now on the subject, I gather wonderful and incredible stories from readers, I seek out the best research and studies that look into the possibility of there being an existence beyond this life. Unlike the other women in my family, I didn't have personal experience of the afterlife until I was well into my thirties, and I've had my fair share of doubt along my own journey. But somehow, I always believed there was something beyond, that our loved ones do look out for us, and sometimes connect with us to help comfort us, give us a boost or occasionally nudge us in the right direction.

There are invisible and in rare cases visible lines of communication between living and dead and this book will illuminate them. However, the book is not just about speaking to and seeing departed loved ones, it is also about how to listen to the voice of heaven in our daily lives. It is about the transformative power of eternal love and a reminder that miracles can and do happen in everyday life. You know that feeling when a bird joins you on your walk, when you pick up the phone to call your loved one and they are already there, or when a stranger is kind just at the moment you needed comfort. These are the moments that bring heaven closer to us.

Since the beginning of time human beings have sought to communicate with departed loved ones, believing that their spirits survive bodily death. The ancient Egyptians believed that death was a transition to a new life, and that if they were judged favourably, then they would be reborn into the afterlife. The ancient Romans believed that this mortal life was only a preparation for the spirit to then take its place in the heavens, the Milky Way. For the Maoris of New Zealand, death traditionally represented a journey and the hope was to be reunited with loved ones who had already made the journey, while Buddhists believe that the soul will be reborn over and over in different bodies. For traditional aborigines, the spirit world was interwoven with the physical world, rather than being two completely separate realms.

In this way, death signified the end of one's physical life, while the spirit would then be released to return to the ancestors and back to the land. Christians have held a variety of beliefs over the centuries about the existence of heaven and hell, the common belief being that there is an afterlife, the question more often being where this might be.

In the past, connecting and communicating with heaven or the afterlife was often an integral part of a culture's customs – but where does that leave us in the modern world? What if you have questions and need the advice of those in spirit? This has been my work for the past two decades, letting people know that the afterlife is real and that there are ways in which we can communicate with heaven when we need guidance, comfort or hope. Spirits do watch over us, or sometimes come to our side with a message or a sign to help us out.

All too often, communicating with heaven is associated with prayer and whenever the word prayer is mentioned the word religion is not far behind – but it has also been my life's work to show that although being religious is a legitimate path to spiritual growth and fulfilment, it is not the only path. Religion and spirituality can be connected but they are not the same thing. In other words, you do not need to be religious to talk to heaven and prayer is not the only way to connect with the other side. All you need is the ability to open your mind, your heart and your eyes to the possibility that this life is not all that there is. If you can do that, heaven will find ways to speak to you.

It is by engaging in conversations, in any kind of communication, that we seek to understand, and in this case we seek to understand the biggest mystery of all, which is death and the possibility of the afterlife. Communication is the process by which we begin to help ourselves make sense of this world and beyond. It is how we connect, and, in some ways, it is when we allow ourselves to really consider death, because we have lost a loved one, that we connect with our own life.

Think of all the varied ways in which we communicate. With words, we might speak to one another, or write or sing. We can communicate through touch, through feelings, intuition or symbols. Think of how much communication there is in our eyes and in a smile. We may simply make a connection or have a conversation with the afterlife quietly in our hearts while we are walking in nature or through a sacred space. We may take a moment at the end of the day or as we open our eyes in the morning to spare a thought for a loved one. We might see something that reminds us of them – a butterfly, a book, the words of a song on the radio. These encounters give us a chance to keep our relationships alive while also allowing ourselves to grieve for the loss.

This book will show you that can you can speak to those on the other side; they can guide and protect you and give you the inspiration you need during difficult times in your life. Contact with spirit can be very healing as it is always loving and good, and also just the belief that we are being watched over is a source of great comfort and support. You will see in these pages that heaven can speak to you and that you can start the conversation too. I hope they may open up more of the world to you and give you extra courage to live the life you dream of.

I hope that by reading this book, and the many wonderful experiences that people send to me, your mind will open up to the possibilities of what the afterlife can offer us. As we open our minds to what *could* be, we are often given a key to our own intuition, we notice the signs put in our path and hear the messages being conveyed to us. A closed mind is a mind that cannot grow or change. An open mind, however, is a transformative mind that can cross the bridge between this life and the next, where time does not exist and life does not end with death.

The types of conversations that we will read about in the following pages are stories of connection and inspiration; they are remembrances. In today's time-poor world, we rush even in our grieving, and we have lost many of our sacred spaces. These stories are reminders to go ahead and give those who have passed from our lives that special time and space in our heart. Thousands of years ago, before the first cities were built, people created spaces where they would commune with the ancestors; this was so they could learn from the spirits, sense their energy and the purpose in their own life. I think that is just what is happening today when people feel a connection with the afterlife. They are sharing a moment, a bond of love, support and memories. When we think of our loved ones who are no longer with us, we think of all the amazing lessons they taught us, and how they would remind us not to take this wonderful chance at life for granted. Through their love, they give us the courage to be ourselves, to try our best, come what may.

So, if you are ready to open your mind and your heart to the possibility of the afterlife and find your own unique way to connect to the world of spirit, let's begin . . .

CHAPTER ONE

Making contact

When hearts listen, heaven sings.
Anonymous

As my readers will know, my belief in heaven is strong but to this day I still have moments of great doubt and times of deep depression when there seems to be no light at the end of the tunnel – no connection to the other side, just silence and emptiness.

My great-aunt, grandmother, mother and brother all had the gift of second sight. I longed to be like them, but however much I studied or absorbed knowledge on the subject, even attending a number of classes to develop my psychic skills, I never saw anything or had any kind of contact with the after-life.

When my mother died, like so many people I was completely unprepared for the loss and the unbearable pain. But rather than allow myself to go through the natural grieving process, I put all my emotional energies into looking for signs from my mother. I knew that death wasn't the end, but I just couldn't understand why she wouldn't come to me or show me in some way that this was the case. I became so fixated that I pushed down my grief and I now realise this was exactly why I wasn't ready to be contacted. At the time I didn't have the awareness to understand this and I felt completely helpless and alone, so much so that I almost lost my beliefs. Because I suppressed my grief rather than accepting it, I was almost overwhelmed by it and found myself in a deep depression.

For anyone who is unfamiliar with depression, it is like falling into a deep, dark hole. Your life becomes a void; it feels like everything is collapsing. For me, there was an overwhelming sense of darkness. Depression is lonely; days go by in slow motion. I felt trapped, as if there was no way out, I lost all my energy and my hopes were replaced by fear and anxiety about every little thing. I was able to hide my pain from others most days, going through the motions, but I was caught in a downward spiral, unable to connect with my life.

And then, my mother paid me a visit in my dreams. All she did was come into my room and tidy it up for me, but how symbolic, as my life was literally in a mess. She looked great – healthy and happy and vital. It was a gentle first contact but incredibly vivid and realistic compared with my usual dreams. It was a dose of comfort that gave me the strength I needed to get up in the morning and begin to turn a corner; to get my life back on track.

I was already a writer by this point in my career, and I'll never know why for sure, but it was at this time that I started to collect afterlife stories and write books about them. The experiences I've been lucky enough to read about in the years since have filled me with joy, hope and continued fascination. And years after that dream visit by my mother she made tangible contact with me for the first time in a night vision. This time she talked to me and I was able to touch her and talk back to her. We had a proper conversation. My mother wanted to let me know that she was always there watching over me and that I must now take the right path.

Just a day later I was driving behind two lorries and as we came up to a junction something told me to go the opposite way, even though it was the wrong direction for my destination. Later that evening I turned on the news to discover the lorries had been in a crash, which had involved the cars behind them too. Very sadly people had died in the crash and I was stunned; something inside me had said to go the other way and this might have saved my life.

From that day I felt that my eyes, my mind and my heart had truly been opened. I was so much more aware of the messages in my dreams and my intuition. I noticed coincidences more and I noticed life more. In its own way, grief so often turns out to be something of a gift in a spiritual sense – it brings us to stillness, sometimes even to our knees, and at the point we reach out genuinely, we begin the conversation.

> *Everything has its wonders, even darkness and silence, and I learn, whatever state I may be in, therein to be content.*
>
> Helen Keller

For me, my impatience growing up, and then putting off my grief in my longing to be contacted by my mother, were blocks to seeing what was right in front of me, that I could simply embrace the fact that celestial beings are all around us and we can talk to them whenever we want. For some people they might actually appear in the traditional angel form, with wings and a halo, or in the forms of departed loved ones. And there are lots of subtler signs too, from white feathers to amazing coincidences, from a thought, a feeling or dream, to a whisper or a touch that comes out of nowhere.

Heaven-sent spirits are also there to help heal and support us in our darker times. Although they are not able to take away all tragedy and pain, they are a reminder of pure goodness and love. Last year I had one of my black times again: when I hear about so much death and cruelty on the news I wonder if I have created a fairy tale. Perhaps the atheists are right, I thought, and my belief in the afterlife a pathetic fantasy. Perhaps all the wonderful experiences or angel-saved-me moments mentioned in my previous books were simply a matter of random chance. This book was due but I could not bring myself to write it. I did not feel worthy. My readers deserved better.

With my children entering their teenage years and the economy so bad, I worried excessively about their future prospects of happiness and success in work and life in an increasingly bleak and depressing world. Coupled with my anxiety about getting older and reaching the big five-o, the darkness I had felt after my mother died was back and I didn't know what to do to pull myself out of its grasp.

With both my parents deceased and never having had close links to other relatives, I had no spiritualist family members to talk to about my doubts and fears and felt increasingly isolated. My husband was a tower of strength but what I needed was some spiritual support. I missed my mother's wisdom and begged for a sign that she was close by but nothing came – this sent me into even deeper depression. Then when I was at the lowest ebb, hope and light returned through a series of wonderful coincidences . . .

It began with a dream: I was back in primary school, aware that the year was 1976. I was looking for my mother but never found her. I did, however, find a room with her name on the door but the name was not her married name, it was her maiden name. When I woke up I could not get the dream out of my head. I found myself idly Googling my old primary school and found mention of it on Friends Reunited. There was a series of photos and I scrolled through and then got the shock of my life when I saw one that was dated 1976. It was a photograph of the staff and there in the front row was the unmistakable face of my mother. She had been a supply teacher at the school on and off for many years, and would not normally have been included in the photos but for some reason that year she was. This was the most amazing shock, as I had never seen the photo before. I have only three or four surviving photos of my mother as, when she died, I was in my early twenties and it was a time of personal poverty and chaos. In the photo she was smiling broadly and I felt that she was sending me a message to let me know she wasn't far away.

The magic of spiritual connection didn't stop there – I went back and thought through every detail of my dream, including the prominent feature of the nameplate using her maiden name. I Googled it and was flabbergasted to find her name on a family tree created by a very distant relative in Holland who was trying to reconstruct his ancestry on the internet. My mum lived and died without the internet, so I had always assumed there was no record of her online. There was an email address, so I got in touch and, to cut a long story short, this person put me in touch with the children of my mother's sister. I knew I had relatives in Holland but as there had been a falling out between my mum and her sister I had never had any contact with them and didn't even know their names. In the space of a week, I went from feeling isolated to being surrounded by five Dutch cousins all keen to make contact and interested in matters spiritual! I wasn't alone. I had family – a huge family – and from beyond the grave Mum had reached out and spoken to me in my dream to let me know that I was part of something bigger and that my life did have meaning and that she was closer to me than ever before.

This remarkable experience fired me up as never before, and after dragging my heels for a year or two with my spiritual writing, it inspired me to finally get down to things and create this book. Throughout my writing sabbatical the letters and emails had continued to pour in and, to my shame, I had not been as diligent in replying as I had in previous years. I stopped delaying and began to reply to them all in earnest. As I read each letter my connection to the world of spirit was renewed and strengthened time and time again. My world felt right again. The people writing to me were like beacons of light and hope – reminding me yet again that heaven exists on earth.

I wanted to write a book to help people going through periods of doubt, isolation and despair similar to the one I had experienced and also to help them discover their own ways to reconnect with heaven. I wanted to publish the many wonderful stories people had continued to send me even when I was doubting myself, as all these stories are amazing reminders that heaven can speak in countless different ways.

About the stories in this book

All the stories are by ordinary people who have had extraordinary experiences. I myself am not a psychic, a medium or an 'angel lady'. I am an ordinary mum of two children who has had some amazing experiences.

I feel very lucky to believe in heaven; to know that every one of us has a guardian angel who watches over us during our life, a source of comfort in dark times, who may shine a light on our thoughts and help us along our path if we have the courage to ask. An open mind and heart dissolve the barrier between heaven and earth; indeed we may be fortunate enough to glimpse a moment of heaven *on* earth – in a fleeting sensation, when we gasp at a coincidence, perhaps as a visitor in our dreams or in signs that cross our path unexpectedly, when we feel protected, encouraged or inspired by a presence not quite of this physical world. This belief is a gift to me.

Here is just one example of when I have been blessed by the presence of heaven in my life. When I was younger I developed an obsession with, or even an addiction to, exercise. It might not sound like something to be very worried about, but it was really beginning to affect my life. Not that I realized that at the time; I felt like exercise was the one thing in my life that I could both rely on and that I could have control over. But in reality it was getting out of control and I was completely dependent on exercise for my self-esteem and to feel okay about the day ahead. I would run for hours, and if for some reason I couldn't run I would spend all my time working out in my head how I would make up for the lost exercise the next day. Like any addiction, I began to need more to feel the same way, until finally I couldn't get the same feelings of being in control because I'd given over responsibility for my sense of self to something that could never make me happy or bring me contentment, however much I thought I wanted it to.

At the height of this obsessive behaviour I was running my usual route in the morning when I had to suddenly stop to tie my laces. I was just by a bench, and sitting there were two women in identical blue coats. I couldn't help but hear one woman say to the other that thank goodness I'd been made to stop by my laces untying, that she wished I would stop more often as I looked miserable when I was running. I was indignant, and put on a big (fake) smile as I ran past them and continued on my way.

The next day I couldn't believe it but my lace came undone at the exact same spot, except this time I didn't see it and took a tumble. A kind man leapt up from the bench and helped me to my feet, guiding me to sit down on the seat and catch my breath. We were sitting just where the two women had been the day before. We got chatting and the man said he also saw me running quite often as he liked to walk early in the morning; he said he thought I must be very disciplined and admired that quality. I told him about the two women from the previous day and how they'd been less than complimentary; as I described how they were wearing identical blue coats he stopped me and looked shocked by what I'd said. 'You know, my wife and her twin sister died in a car accident together and they always wore the same blue coats. You must be a messenger, chosen to let me know that they are here with me in some way and that they're clearly okay! This is such a gift, thank you.'

The man looked so at peace – what a great moment here on earth. And I decided to listen to the message for me, too. I walked home that day and took my time to look at my surroundings with open eyes once again, rather than running blindly past everything. In time I was able to be much more balanced about my health and exercise and it turns out that I started to smile a lot more too – not with my teeth but with my heart. I stopped constantly searching for happiness on the outside and began to notice it within. There was a great deal of pain there too, but I began to let myself heal, I began to let go of my old ideas of perfection and replaced self-criticism with more acceptance and love. I'll never forget how a message from heaven helped me to begin to change my life that day. These are the moments when things shift, when we discover a sense of freedom and embrace the potential for life to be transformed. Spiritual development is, after all, development of the self.

It is a common and understandable mistake to think that you need to be psychic or have a special gift to communicate with heaven, but heaven can be glimpsed by anyone. Heaven does not discriminate! All of the people who have sent their stories are ordinary people with ordinary lives and a number of them were not even religious or spiritual before their experience – but something extraordinary happened to convince them that heaven spoke to them and changed their lives for ever and all wanted their stories to be shared with my readers in the hope that they would offer comfort, hope, inspiration and guidance. All of the stories are to the best of my knowledge true accounts – I have no reason to doubt the honesty of the people who write to me. Some stories have been edited and names changed if personal identity needs to be protected or I felt strongly that it would be best to give another name due to the personal nature of the experiences, but all the accounts are real and true as far as I know.

A time for heaven

There is a time for all things and never has the time been so right for heaven to reveal itself and reach out to us than right now. I have been gathering stories of experiences with angels and the spirit world for many years and have noticed how it seems to be a growing movement, even in an era when we might think that science and reason would be more likely to be gaining ground over faith and mystery. While there has been a decline in religion I think there has been a surge in spiritual hunger, a desire to find the meaning, goodness and love in our world during such turbulent times. For me, it's almost like the spirits have launched a concerted campaign; they know the time is right. So if we are ever feeling confused, lonely or fearful we can remember pure spiritual beings are right there with us, surrounding us with love and compassion.

I find it fascinating even how readers are often guided to my books in mysterious ways – as a gift or left on the Tube or in a library when they are searching for something else. Each person reading this book is meant to be reading this book.

About this book

Working on this book has once again renewed and revitalized my connection to the world of spirit and helped me look back on my life again and realize that even though I thought heaven wasn't with me it was there all along – I just didn't know how to recognize it. I sincerely hope that reading this book will help you recognize when heaven is calling and serve as a catalyst for your belief by showing you that anyone can open their heart and their mind and hear the voice of heaven loud and clear.

The chapters that follow in this book will explore some of the awe-inspiring stories about communicating with the other side that have been sent to me in recent years. There will also be advice about how to recognize, talk to and, most important of all, listen to heaven. Chapters Two to Five will look at perhaps the most common ways heaven can speak to us and those are through our intuition, our dreams and through coincidences and signs, and, in rare cases, visions of angels and spirits. Each chapter will be punctuated with stories from my readers. Chapter Six, however, will turn the spotlight on you. This chapter will look at how you can have your own conversations with heaven. I have written this especially for those who feel they haven't caught a glimpse of heaven yet and don't understand why.

Anyone, whatever their age, background, religious beliefs or lack of them, can catch a glimpse of heaven on earth. This isn't a privilege reserved for the select few, or the most devout, religious or pure! All of us are born with the ability to see spirit in one way or another if we know how and where to look. Think of this book as your guide – where we shall highlight some of the signposts that it is possible to use as pointers to heaven.

> *I'm trying to free your mind, Neo. But I can only show you the door. You're the one who has to walk through it.*
>
> Morpheus, *The Matrix*

CHAPTER TWO

When heaven speaks

Our lives begin to end the day we become silent about things that matter.

Anonymous

Communication is how we connect; it is how we understand each other and guide each other. Of course, the most obvious way we communicate is through language, in particular speech, but there are so many ways in which we are able to have conversations with heaven. We may connect through our dreams; sometimes heaven leaves signs for us through objects like feathers, through animals and birds who come to our side, or through coincidences. Sometimes the conversation takes place deep within ourselves – suddenly we feel a heightened sense of intuition or that we seem to have direct access to our wisdom, lighting our path for us.

In this chapter we will explore some of more common ways

to hear heaven speak and how you can gain inspiration to move forward by listening to and talking to the world of spirit. There are the times when people experience an incredibly dramatic divine intervention and believe that their lives or the lives of those close to them have been saved by some kind of sign or message from heaven. And then there are the many more subtle ways in which we might have our attention caught by a message from heaven; when heaven speaks to us through intuition, coincidences and in answer to our prayers or questions.

What is consistent throughout all types of heavenly communication is that underlying it all is a language based on love. Feelings are the primary language of celestial beings. When heaven reaches out to touch us in some way, we often feel an emotional embrace. We feel safe and peaceful; our inner strength, confidence and courage are nourished. We might sense the presence of spirits giving us a helping hand, or we might suddenly have a moment of pure clarity, a flash of insight that means we know which direction to go in. As we reach out through our prayers, by which I don't automatically mean religious prayers, but simply when we ask for help or send out our love to others in need, we may receive an answer in the form of a good friend turning up on our doorstep, or in a sentence that stares us in the face as a book falls open. There are so many ways for heaven to send us a message; we're watching, listening and in touch with all our senses so that we might be open to receiving a bit of heavenly help.

There are many well-known stories of people being saved by heaven or visited by spirits or heavenly guides, of people surviving against all human odds. I would like to share some of the stories that might not have been reported in the papers but that have been sent to me by everyday people over the years. To me, they show how the most extraordinary things can happen to any one of us. These types of experiences are rare, and heaven is much more likely to speak with us in more subtle ways, such as through coincidences and help that suddenly appears, as if out of nowhere. But I do find these stories so uplifting and inspiring that I wanted to share a couple with you now.

One of the most intriguing stories I was sent a few years ago came from a gentleman called Arnie:

A silver gift from my twin

I am writing to tell you about the time I nearly died.

When I was thirty-three, I was diagnosed with colon cancer. I had begun to notice very early signs in my late twenties. I had been a really athletic person, a keen runner and weekend footballer; I had even run a few marathons. But I had started to feel less well and began to have minor problems 'down there'; as a typical man I was too embarrassed to go to my doctor and also I tended to dismiss my symptoms as probably being haemorrhoids or something like that. It was only when the pain continued to get worse that I knew something could be seriously wrong. Unfortunately by the time I was diagnosed, the cancer had already spread to my liver and I was given only six months to a year to live.

As a young man, I had always thought I was invincible and I just didn't know how to handle this kind of news. I found myself in full-blown denial, trying to carry on as if nothing had changed. But I was very ill – quickly I became so frail that the inevitable happened and I was taken into hospital. I didn't cope well with being faced by such a grim reality so suddenly and I sank into depression. Any fight to survive that had been with me up until that point just drained away, I couldn't even face being visited by family and friends as I had no brave face to put on the situation.

So you see, I wasn't one of those people you read about who show amazing courage when faced with their own death. I was scared, lonely and even managed to push away the very people who loved me and wanted to be there to support and care for me. I felt like death would be a release from all the distress for everyone; I would even go to sleep longing not to wake up the next day, and as I did awake tears would fall down my cheeks as I just didn't know how to face the day.

Then one day, as I lay awake in my hospital bed, something I believe to be incredible happened. A man who I had never seen but vaguely recognized as he looked a little bit like me walked into my room. I just thought he was a nurse; he busied himself tidying the room a bit before he came to sit on the edge of my bed. He sat there for a while, then delved into his pockets and produced a little silver angel figure, which he gave to me. He told me that I should hold on to it whenever I was feeling lost or without hope, and then he left.

Just then, a nurse I recognized came in. She must have seen the strange man and so I asked her if she knew him.

She looked at me like I was daft – surely it was my brother, she said, he looked exactly like me. Well, I couldn't get him out of my head all day, and later that evening when my mother noticed the little angel on the bedside table I told her about the strange events of the day. She went white as a sheet as I described how the nurse assumed we were brothers, we looked so alike. I asked her what was wrong and after a deep breath she told me a piece of news she had kept from me my whole life out of kindness and wanting to protect me. I had had a twin brother, who died only minutes after we were born. My mother had been a twin herself, and her sister too had died at birth. She had known about her twin and as this knowledge had always been such a great source of grief and guilt to her, she had wanted to spare me from the same pain.

It was an extraordinary turning point for me. I can't explain exactly what happened, but from that day my mental focus changed and my health began to improve. I held on to that little angel every time I felt in need of support or courage. I started to engage in the healing process and began to practise visualization, began to get out of bed more often and try to eat to help improve my strength.

A few months later I had all the usual checks and tests. I was used to these appointments and previously all the doctor could do was to tell me they would keep doing whatever was possible, while looking apologetic. This time was different. The doctor looked confused, but there was a different glimmer in his eye. A second doctor was called in to check all the test results. Tell me what's the matter, I said, whereupon they told me that was the thing, they couldn't find anything wrong at all.

The cancer had gone. The doctors called it 'spontaneous regression', which is really another way of saying 'miracle'.

By his own admission, Arnie was a regular guy; he was a football-playing young man who was terrified by his illness and was beginning to isolate himself even from those who loved him a great deal. This is a story of amazing transformation, the theme that runs throughout this book and the incredible stories within. Even in our darkest moments, and this was the darkest time imaginable for Arnie in his young life, there is the potential for love to enter and give us the courage to act or think differently. Through his brother's visit and gift, Arnie found the inner strength to take a completely different emotional, mental and physical approach to his illness.

Perhaps Arnie's brother was there to tell him that it didn't need to be his time yet. At other times, the appearance of spirits or angels – which in my mind are one and the same thing – is a reassuring sign that it's okay to embrace death when it is the right time. There is a lovely passage in Elisabeth Kübler-Ross's book *On Grief and Grieving* in which a woman who is very ill in hospital tells her husband that she is happy because she has just talked with heavenly guides. The doctor takes this news badly, saying, 'That's never a good sign,' while the hospital chaplain thinks that spiritually, it is the *best* sign. Just as Arnie's angel gave him a helping hand back towards his life, our angels are also there to guide us from this life into the next.

Irina felt that her life was saved by an unseen hand as she was pulled under by a strong wave while on holiday in Italy.

Lifted above the waves

I'm writing to tell you about an episode that took place when I was at the seaside in Talamone in Tuscany, Italy. I was fifteen and every morning I would swim in the sea. On this particular morning, like every other, I was ready at the same place to go in the water. That day the sea was very bad, and I could see there were a lot of waves; my dad told me to be sure to be extra careful while I was swimming.

As I was playing with the waves, suddenly a really big wave came out of nowhere. I couldn't jump above it and it dragged me under the surface. It kept pulling me further down, I wasn't able to get back to the surface and my breath was beginning to run out. At first I panicked, but as my oxygen was almost completely gone my mind couldn't think any more. I opened my eyes and waited for my fate, giving myself to the sea.

In that moment I saw under the sea a shape coming my way and it seemed to give me its hand. I took it and the shape gently brought me back safely to the surface. I took a gulp of air and regained my strength. As I got out of the water and walked up onto the beach, I felt safe and stronger than the sea.

That experience made me understand that nothing is impossible. Many people look for miracles to believe in something – instead I think that miracles happen every day in normal life; you only need to have a free heart and to be full of charity and you will soon notice them.

Like many others who have felt a similar presence during a time of great danger, Irina took a wonderful message from her experience in that she now sees miracles all around her in everyday, 'normal' life. Her eyes and her heart had been completely opened by what happened.

Sophia also feels very comforted when she remembers the time when heaven caught her as she fell.

A gentle landing

A few years after my husband left me I found a new home. The first evening I moved in, I was busy home-making late into the evening and I stood on the kitchen units to put up some curtains. I stepped backwards and fell back onto the stone floor. However, as I fell it seemed to happen in slow motion. I'm a big girl and when I fall I go with a thud, but I just landed gently on my back without a scratch on me. I often ask myself, did someone lower me to the ground? In my heart it feels like someone was there, supporting me.

When I was a child I was interested in 'the lady in the curtains' or the faces in the kitchen tiles. I was interested in spiritual things but then gradually I lost this part of my life, especially now that I am studying sociology at university. I've always battled with depression – life has been quite hard and it feels like my heart has hardened with it, it's like I have stopped allowing myself to hope that I might find love, like I have pulled down the emotional shutters. But remembering what happened that evening reminds me of the times when my faith has given me comfort and that I might open my heart and mind to the love that is all around us.

I know exactly what Sophia means when she finds emotional support within the physical sensation of being gently supported down to the ground when she falls. There is a team-bonding exercise that involves allowing yourself to fall backwards knowing that your colleagues or friends will be right there behind you to catch you as you fall, keeping you safe. It's almost as if Sophia's heavenly guides were doing just that as she fell back off the kitchen units. Her team was right there, both to catch her and to support her when life gets very hard.

In the following story, Seósamh also felt the protective hand of heavenly beings on two separate occasions, once as a small child but then again as an adult while driving. I, too, have felt guided while driving.

A helping hand of protection

I bought your book *Celtic Angels* and I am contacting you as you continue to take an interest in carrying out research into the paranormal and invited a response to that effect.

I have had two separate experiences in life involving my guardian angel, one as a young child and the other as an adult. The first experience, like the second, was brief and to the point.

I was hopping on the bed with my brother Christy at our

home in Kilrush as a young child in early 1960 when an angel's hand appeared on the outside of the bed. This resulted in me stopping hopping. I remember looking under the bed immediately afterwards but there was nobody there. The only explanation I have is that the angel's hand prevented me from accidentally falling onto the floor and was alerting me to take care.

The second occasion happened many years later, possibly in 1996 or thereabouts, late at night as I was driving along a familiar road between Roscrea and Templemore, North Tipperary. An angel's hand appeared to the left of my hand, parallel with the steering wheel. It was a brief but real experience. I have often wondered why it appeared to me. I put it down to my guardian angel protecting me. I arrived safe at my usual destination within twenty minutes.

The hand was the colour of my own white skin in both instances. It was a definitely a pretty, lady's hand without clothing or rings or bracelets. I estimate that the hand was about sixteen inches in length but I can't be exact. In my estimation it was the same hand I witnessed as a child.

Annie wrote to me to share two experiences she had as a teenager.

Someone stopped me

When I was thirteen, I was on my way to school. We'd just bought a new car and my dad was dropping me and my friend off. My brother, who was ten at the time, was there too.

We'd stopped at a junction and were just about to turn onto the road to the school when another car sped through a red light and hit us. My side, the passenger side, had the most extensive damage but I got out and, even in shock, I felt myself being guided away from the crash. I was pulled out of school later on and told that we were lucky it wasn't in our old car, otherwise I wouldn't be here. My mum said it was my guardian angel and I'm inclined to believe her.

Another thing that happened, which highlighted my guardian angel's presence, was when I was sixteen and in a really dark place. I had huge exams that year in school and I'd lost my granny that Christmas, before the mocks took place. I was very tempted to take my own life, I'd even written a note. But when it came to it, something, or rather someone, stopped me and I tore up the note. I started counselling then and the night before my exams, my granny appeared. All she did was smile at me but I felt much more relaxed about them.

In her darkest moment, Annie was given the strength to turn back from her fears and then seek out professional help through counselling. It is lovely to see that her grandmother then appears to give extra reassurance through a smile, which must be the perfect message of comfort that you could receive from heaven.

Mirabel, too, felt that she was saved when she had lost all hope.

The day heaven saved me

It was coming up to Father's Day and our two daughters had surprised their dad with tickets to an air show near our home. That morning he and I set off for the show and on arrival we set up our chairs and picnic, all ready to enjoy the display. The Red Arrows were going to be performing the finale, something we were really looking forward to, but then at around two o'clock, halfway through the display, I had a desperate desire to go home. My husband pleaded for us to stay and see the Red Arrows but my feelings were so strong that I became quite emotional and so we left the show early and returned home.

When we arrived, our younger daughter was waiting there for us and immediately told us that my brother had been in a motorcycle accident. This was before mobile phones and so she had had no way of reaching us at the air show. She was waiting for more news about which hospital he had been taken to. Just a few moments later our phone rang and it was my other brother. He said for me to sit down, so I knew it was going to be bad news; my brother had not only been in an accident but he had been killed. They estimated that he died at around 2 p.m.

Following the death of my brother I experienced a very stressful and traumatic time. I reached breaking point, and one day when my daughters and husband were out for the day I drove my car into the forest, drank a bottle of brandy and attached a rubber tube to the exhaust. I put a brick on the accelerator, put the tube through the window and lay down on the back seat, thinking I was ready to give up.

An elderly couple who lived a little way away from the area had been asked by their daughter to come and check on her pony that weekend, but they couldn't find the pony and so ended up wandering further afield through the forest. They spotted my car in the clearing and then the pony appeared at the same moment on the other side amongst the trees. As they approached the pony they suddenly realized the situation and they smashed the windows of the car, pulling me out unconscious. I spent several days in intensive care and then months in a psychiatric hospital. This was almost twenty years ago and today I live a wonderful life with a beautiful grandson and a loving family around me. I know heaven saved me that day – my time hadn't come.

Mirabel's story of tragedy, followed by transformation after the day she was saved by the couple looking for their pony, is inspiring and hopeful. She ends her letter with a description of her life today, full of love, which is after all the language of heaven.

Intuition

Angels are intelligent reflections of light, that original light which has no beginning. They can illuminate. They do not need tongues or ears, for they can communicate without speech, in thought.

John of Damascus

One of the most powerful but often neglected ways to converse with heaven is through intuition. Accessing our 'inner guide' helps us to know if we are on the right path. I believe it is a nudge from the other side that gives us the courage and confidence to listen to and act upon our intuition. We might experience a flash of insight or a moment of quiet, calm knowing. I'm often asked if this isn't just us being in touch with our own instincts, but for me I believe there are definite times when we know there is something more than this. It almost feels as though someone is there to hold our hand – we might even feel this as a physical sensation, or simply a strong sense that we are being emotionally supported.

These are the moments when heavenly beings are giving us a helping hand. In these moments we feel completely safe – safe enough to let go and trust ourselves, our decisions and our actions. We open ourselves up to our wisdom and inner strength. Most of the time, our minds are rushing all over the place, searching for the answers to our problems here, there and everywhere. And then suddenly, everything becomes calm and quiet, we feel like we're completely tuned in, and we just know what we need to do.

We might think of these sensations as 'gut feelings', 'instincts' or our 'sixth sense'. These are all good ways of describing them, and it's good to go with what feels right to us. These are the moments when we feel connected to something that is beyond our own usual sense of reasoning and logic. We no longer have to endlessly weigh up the pros and cons of a decision, we are no longer paralysed by our fears of getting it wrong, not being perfect or worrying about all the what-ifs.

An excellent way to help ourselves tune into our intuition is by practising and developing our sense of empathy, which is our ability to sense what others are feeling through our loving concern for them. Being able to empathise with others takes connection and communication. You know how sometimes a person you are with is all smiles but you can sense their hidden pain underneath. As we become more in tune with the feelings of others we likewise become more in tune with the language of heaven, so, just as we might be a kind stranger to others in times of need, we will be equally open to the kindness strangers, and angels, are looking to show to us.

Intuition is often accompanied by the sensation of a presence, somehow recognizing the essence of a departed loved one or a feeling of being guided or simply embraced. The purpose of this presence might be reassurance that your loved ones are still with you in some way, or there might be a helpful message in the presence which can guide you to where you need to be in your life.

Sensing the presence of a departed loved one is incredibly comforting. Many children are unself-conscious about having invisible friends but as we grow up we lose touch with our natural psychic powers. As humans we are social creatures and it makes sense that in spirit we continue to feel compelled to communicate.

The following story was sent to me by Charlotte, and is a powerful example of how a divine message came through to her through her own intuition.

Heaven on my shoulder

While on holiday in Majorca I booked a day trip to the local market with a coach party. Before I boarded the coach I called at the shop for a newspaper. But I didn't just buy a newspaper – I found myself buying medical wipes, lint, small scissors and a roll of plasters. I had no idea why, it felt like someone was telling me to do this.

When I was walking through the market later that morning I heard an old lady crying and in shock behind me. Her leg was bleeding quite badly, so I sat her down on the wall and tended her injury. A stallholder nearby gave her a sip of brandy to calm her nerves. As I left them and walked on I said thank you to the celestial being or angel on my shoulder that day.

You may notice that I like to use the word angel interchangeably with the words spirit or celestial being. In the strict sense angels are not spirits – in that angels are pure beings that have not lived on earth whereas spirits are the pure energy manifestations of departed loved ones – but in my mind there is no difference as both are heaven-sent and both bring the same message of goodness, comfort, hope and love.

Josephine experienced a physical sensation that prevented her from changing lanes at the precise moment a car was in her blind spot.

Driving in the dark

I was driving in the dark on a busy dual carriageway. I needed to pull over into the outside lane, and thought it was clear so I went to turn the steering wheel and move over. My hands just froze on the steering wheel; I couldn't turn it. Thank goodness, as there was a car in my blind spot at that very moment. When it passed I was able to steer again.

Harry listened to his inner voice or spirit when he heard a message in the middle of the night.

An impulse purchase

Eighteen months ago I began to be worried about the development of arthritis in one of my ankles; this concerned me in case it might cause difficulties driving. I was awoken one night by a voice saying, 'Get an automatic car.' I couldn't get to sleep again all night and after breakfast, as though in a dream, I drove to the Toyota garage and said to the salesman, 'Do you have an Aygo automatic?' He replied that they happened to have just one, which was about a year and a half old. I went for a quick test drive and agreed there and then to trade in my existing car for a part-exchange deal. This must have been one of the quickest sales that salesman had ever made! Even now, I can't believe I did it with so little consideration, but it was exactly the car

I needed, my decision spurred on by that voice that woke me up in the middle of the night!

There are times when we simply feel a presence. We know that someone isn't physically there, but we sense them all the same. This is what happened to Yasmin, who felt her dad at the celebration of her daughter's confirmation.

I'm so glad Dad was there, too

When my daughter was confirmed we had invited family and friends along to the church to share the occasion with us. It was a happy day, except we very much missed my dad, who had passed away only a short time before. My daughter was extremely close to her 'Grandy' (as she called him) and she meant the whole world to him. I remember standing by the altar that day, thinking how proud and pleased Dad would have been, when I had the feeling he was behind me looking over my left shoulder. I was so convinced he was there I turned round to look; of course he wasn't there in body but I believe he wanted me to know he was present.

Coincidences

Another time-honoured way to communicate with spirit is to tune into the coincidences in your life. Alongside intuition, coincidences are a common way for heaven to speak to us. Many people will dismiss these moments as *just* coincidence', i.e. that they can be explained by complete random chance and that there is nothing to read into them. I believe if we dismiss coincidences then we are throwing away a wonderful gift that might just be a message from heaven. I'm not alone when I say that many coincidences feel like so much more. They are moments that re-connect us with the wonder of life, and the wonder of what we might not see or understand but that we somehow feel.

Researchers have discovered that people who think they are more lucky turn out to actually *be* more lucky – it's as though being more optimistic and open to chance going their way brings more luck into their life. Just as luck isn't as random as we first might think, I believe the same is true for coincidences and synchronicity. If we are open to the positive feelings these experience can give us then we are more likely to experience them.

I get a warm, almost magical feeling when a coincidence crosses my path. That moment of synchronicity when you think of a friend you haven't seen for ages and then the phone rings and it's them on the other end of the line. I'm always amazed when I bump into people I know when I'm on holiday or on a packed Tube carriage, in amongst literally millions of Londoners. What are the chances? And then there are the times when we have been wrangling with a question or a dilemma and suddenly the answer is staring us in the face as a book opens to a page with a sentence that immediately speaks directly to our inner wisdom. It happened again when I was working on this book. Just as I was getting the final draft ready to send to my editor and worrying and wondering if in our increasingly cynical, materialist world a book about spiritual growth would be well received, a leading national newspaper ran a series of lengthy features every day of the week about near-death experiences. It felt as if heaven was saying – look, everybody wants to talk about the afterlife.

As well as calls out of the blue or spotting a familiar face on a beach in Mexico, there are the moments of serendipity that again help to give us a guiding hand with the right direction in our life, or help us to be of help to others. We find ourselves asking what on earth made us happen to be in exactly the right place at the right split second in time.

I believe that coincidences are often a message sent to encourage us to pay attention in our lives and during our everyday experiences. They are so special that they feel like a reminder to always live in the moment so that we might notice everything that is magical, good and loving around us. We are encouraged to develop our awareness, so that we may connect more with our own inner wisdom and also with others. We may become more open to opportunities, noticing them when they are there in front of us, and not afraid to grab them. We may become more open to the big, divine plan of our life, and appreciative of everything we have right now, especially all the things we give and receive through love.

For Joe, it was a near miss that brought home just how precious life is and how sometimes, for reasons unknown to us, it just isn't our time to go.

The day I didn't start work

The most startling incident happened about three years ago and it was a time when I was in the process of changing my job. I had applied for and succeeded in getting a job with a local man who ran a security alarm business with his partner.

To make a long story short, we had arranged to meet up on the Monday to allow him to train me for the next three days. This would include calling on households and commercial outlets to generate business, as my job would be to sell the alarm products and the two owners of the business would then complete the installations.

However, as my son was starting college in a different area that same week I needed to be at home to help him to move. It would take us a few days to get everything packed and ready, and so I arranged with my new employers to start later in the week instead of the Monday.

So Monday was busy for us at home and on Tuesday I decided to ring my new boss to check in. I rang him at around 12.30 but the phone kept ringing and eventually went to voicemail. I left a message that I'd be in touch again to arrange when I would be starting work and the areas I'd be working in. Just a few hours later that same afternoon I got the shock of my life when I heard on local radio that there had been an accident at 11.20 a.m. that morning and that a person had died. I don't know how but I just knew immediately that it was my boss, although it wasn't confirmed until later that evening who the person was.

I was in complete shock at the realization that had it not been for my son starting college and needing my help, I was meant to be in his car with him on that morning. I find this unnerving, but also that it feels like someone was looking out for me – that it wasn't my time for whatever reason. I thank heaven I know I'm not any different to anyone else but I guess I'm still here for a reason. Things like this have happened to me before and I can tell you that I'm starting to feel like the cat with nine lives! I hope you find my experiences of near misses interesting and revealing and indeed positive in that I'm here to relate these stories.

I had to smile at Susanna's story, which follows. She wrote to tell me about the coincidence that led to her reading one of my books, and also to share an experience while driving when she heard a shout out of nowhere that brought her to her senses and made her able to regain control of her car.

This book is for me

I'm from Porto, Portugal, I'm thirty-eight years old and I'd like to tell you my story of how your book *How to See Angels* came into my hands so that I would have the opportunity to read it.

In June of this year I received a registered letter notification. I had missed the postman and so had seven days to go to the post office and collect the letter. But the seven days passed and I still hadn't gone to get it. After three weeks I remembered the letter, and although I knew it would no longer be at the post office, 'something' told me that I should still go there. So I did!

When I arrived at the post office, there were a few people in the queue ahead of me so I began to look through the books that were on sale there. I picked up your book and as soon as I started to read the first lines, I said to myself, 'This book is for me.'

When my turn arrived, I presented the ticket and the girl told me that my letter was no longer there. I smiled as of course I knew it, but I went ahead and bought your book. I read it in three days during my holidays, lying on the beach. I loved it. I was at a phase in my life where I had so many doubts about so many things but I knew I was meant to read your book and another one from Portugal that is similar. These two books reignited my motivation and belief to continue my spiritual journey. I smiled as long as I read your book.

I'd like to tell you another story now about the angels. When I was about twenty-two years old I was driving my car with three friends. Suddenly at a curve of the road, I lost control of the car. I felt paralysed and I had no reaction. But I heard a shout and this suddenly made me put my foot on the brake and regain control of the car. When we stopped, I asked my friends which of them had shouted and they each answered, 'It wasn't me.' I was so sure that I heard a shout and this had helped me in that instant to get control of the situation, preventing us from crashing. Now I feel sure it was my spirit guide. Sometimes my angels talk to me while I'm sleeping and give me the answers to my doubts in my dreams. It is a great feeling.

Heather, too, experienced a helpful moment of synchronicity when she opened a copy of one of my books to a random page.

Shared experiences

It was really kind of you to send me a signed copy of your book *An Angel Saved Me*. I opened it at random to page 204 to the story about the girl who took seven paracetamol tablets and lost her sight. I took a deliberate overdose myself back in 1982, of fifty paracetamol and aspirin. It was my second attempt at suicide. In November 1981, when I was nineteen, I took an overdose of an antidepressant drug. I went to work as normal. While I was sitting alone in my partitioned-off section of the large open plan office, I saw before me, building up slowly, the figures of my deceased mother and grandfather. I could only describe them as 'beings of light', not a term I was familiar with back then. They were quite firm and I was impressed with the knowledge that 'it was not time yet' and I was to 'go back as I had work to do'. I knew they did not mean my work at the engineering firm. I also believe they helped me years later in sorting out a house for me and a means of support as they knew without this I was not likely to want to continue my time on earth.

Sarah also felt that heavenly guides were at work when circumstances conspired to help find her new job.

With a little help from the other side

I was reading one of your books and your lovely stories of how heaven has touched the lives of so many people. I believe my angels also touched my life, and I would like to tell you the story of how I got my new job and how I feel my angels played a part in this.

I had taken voluntary redundancy and had been looking for a job for just over a month. My friend came round to my house to look for jobs online, and after a while I told her to come out into the garden for a break. We started talking about my garden and how I wanted to put up some different fencing. My friend said her neighbour Jill had the fencing I wanted and that she was getting rid of it, she probably didn't want anything for it either, so I said would she mind if I went round later that evening and picked it up. I did and while we were talking, Jill said there was a job going at her place. I asked if she would mind getting me a job application form, to which she replied, yes of course. Well, this was on Wednesday, and Jill brought home an application form the next day, I filled it out and the next Tuesday the HR person called me to ask for me to go to an interview the following day. So just a week later I went for an interview, and unbelievably they offered me the job first thing Thursday.

It seems so strange – I had wanted to get my fencing for over a year and I could have bought it at any time so what had been stopping me?

This life-changing event took only a week and I believe it

was thanks to my angels. I later found out that the job hadn't been advertised anywhere: it felt like I was meant to find out about it and get the job. Oh, and my garden looks fab too!

I strongly believe the more people who read your wonderful books and the wonderful stories in them, the quicker we can empower people to believe in their own angels and turn this world around for the better.

For Steph, a coincidence happened just as she was reading one of my previous books.

What are the odds?

Last night I was reading your book *The Afterlife Is Real*. With my husband tucked up in bed, I had got to the piece about things being moved. I thought to myself, 'Oh I know what my husband would move if he had passed over.' It would be a figurine I have of an upright dog with worn-out clothes, about six inches from top of shabby hat to toe, with a terrible hangdog expression on its face. And then an uninvited thought jumped in, saying, 'But I would easily find an explanation for it being moved.'

I left your book with one more chapter to read and took myself to bed. Turning back the covers I thought, 'No, it can't be,' but it there it was, my treasured tramp dog lying on my pillow. My husband had put him there after seeing him tucked behind some books.

What are the odds?

How would I explain that away?
Why would I want to?

Steph could hardly believe it, but it's wonderful that instead of trying to explain it away she embraces this little moment of synchronicity.

Right place, right time

I remember a reader writing to me once about all the times he felt that heaven had somehow led him to be in the right place at the right time, often there just at the moment a person needed catching as they fell, or needed help in an emergency. It does feel at times like this that more than just lucky coincidence is at play: it's as though events come together to put us in exactly the place we need to be in order to help or support someone in their moment of need.

There are also the times when things seem to be going very badly, but then turn out for the best in the end. We might think of this as simply being able to see the silver lining of a situation, although to me even the description of a cloud's 'silver lining' speaks in the language of spirits, when events seem to conspire to show us a glimpse of heaven just when we are about to write off a day in the hope that tomorrow might prove a better one.

This was just the case for Dalma, who was visiting the UK from Hungary, and discovered the unpredictable nature of our country buses.

Village of angels

A very special story has happened to me in England, so special that I was sure that I would write about it in some way and share it with others. My name is Dalma and I am thirty-two years old. I am a Hungarian, with a legal background, and I have always been quite a spiritual person since I was a child. I believe that I was only able to come through and survive my difficult childhood and teenage years with the help of angels from another world. Anyway, I have lived in Malta for the past year and a half, and while here I have been practising yoga as a friend taught me some of the movements and meditation. These practices help me very much in times of loneliness. I have even begun to learn about something called Deeksha energy, which I feel has helped to open me up and strengthen my energies.

The following experience happened while I was visiting the UK – I feel this trip was a gift to me. It was my last day in Cheltenham, a spring day in March. I was visiting my friends in the UK, as many Hungarians live and work there. My friend Márti lives in Cheltenham and works as a software tester and team leader at a computer company; his fiancée is a journalist working for the Cheltenham and Gloucester papers. They were so nice to me and showed me many places to visit. One of these places was Bourton-on-the-Water, which is in the Cotswolds. The only thing that I knew about the village was that it has a small river and it is called the Venice of the Cotswolds.

As it was my last day with Márti and his fiancée, I took my morning a bit easy, and so I started my day trip from Up Hatherley and through Cheltenham a little later than I had planned. Also the Cheltenham horse races were on, which caused great traffic on the roads. Eventually I reached the main bus station and found the bus to Bourton-on-the-Water. After forty minutes, and only seeing highways and fields, I decided to get off at Northleach as it was the stop just before Bourton-on-the-Water. I told the driver I would stop off there and look around a bit, thinking I would be able to walk to the next village. Little did I know I was still seven miles away from the English Venice. In a restaurant they printed out a map, but really did not recommend walking along the highway as there were cars passing that would be going seventy miles an hour. And according to the timetable there was a bus due in an hour, so it might be better to wait and catch that. It was really starting to get quite late in the afternoon, though, and I was a bit fed up but determined to get to Bourton-on-the-Water. I can't think why but I decided to hitchhike, something I wouldn't recommend but I was so adamant about reaching my destination. I started towards the main road and then suddenly the bus drove past. I didn't wave or try to stop it, who knows why. As soon as it had disappeared I berated myself for being stupid – it was so typical of me. I was starting to feel sorry for myself – why did I always make situations harder for myself? Cars were passing me and none were stopping. I wasn't sure what on earth I should do.

I was just starting to panic and feel very worried when

suddenly a dark blue Land Rover was coming towards me. As it reached me I wished hard that it would stop but it continued past. The car was going in the opposite direction to me, but something made me turn around and then I saw that it had stopped. A friendly looking man was driving with a small baby in a car seat next to him. As the man opened the door, the baby dropped her toy and it landed on the concrete. I picked it up and asked the man if he might be able to give me a lift to Bourton-on-the-Water, to which he replied it was no problem, it was on his way. The baby was so cute and blonde; she had started crying a bit, but stopped when I handed her back her little toy.

As I got into the car, 'Angels' by Robbie Williams started playing on the radio. I was speechless – there was something special in the air at that moment. As we drove down and then up a steep valley I realized I would never had made the journey on foot. It would have taken me hours, but in the car we were there in ten minutes. What a relief! I thanked the man for helping me out, and I said no wonder 'Angels' was playing on the radio.

I took a deep breath and was able to calm down, and as I did I was amazed by the beauty and peace of this small village and its river. I began to take photos and then as I reached the little high street I went into the first shop I came across. It was a perfumery and they were just about to start a free tour, so I stayed for the tour and learnt all about how they made the fragrances. After that I had something to eat, by which time I had an hour left before the last bus would return to Cheltenham.

I wanted to get an impression of the village and so I began to walk. I found another calling place for my heart, which is called the Little Nook. This shop had an amazing atmosphere, with elegant, small souvenirs inside, such as wind bells with butterflies and hearts, special handcrafts, colouring books for children, spiritual cards and angel cards. I went into the shop because outside there was a small stand with wind bells and one of them was the same colour as the shutter on my balcony in Budapest. It caught my attention and I decided to buy it. I then saw a book with the title *Angel Babies*. It was a lovely coincidence as I felt the child in the car had been like an 'angel baby', helping me out through her father. On the cover of the book the baby had the same blue eyes with long eyelashes and blondish locks as the baby in the car.

I felt and was sure that Bourton-on-the-Water is a village of angels. I told this to one of the shop assistants, that an amusement park had nothing compared with this. He laughed hard.

I started to read the book right away on the way back to Cheltenham and there in the introduction was an email address where angel stories are welcome. I hope the angels will continue to help me. I love England and I appreciate all that love and help that I received on this small journey and adventure. I learnt a great deal and appreciate that I have experienced something unique and spiritual.

It's not just kind strangers who seem to appear just at the right moment, but also objects, especially books, that present themselves to us when we need them. Many people write to me with fascinating stories about how they first discovered my books, and how often they feel a huge sense of relief and also joy to then realize just how many people have had similar experiences to them, that they don't have to feel odd or alone. This in turn is a great comfort and inspiration to me, to know that by bringing people's stories together the books bring people together in spirit.

Prayer

In many religions talking to heaven is something that is done through prayer. And while I tend not to focus on the religious, ritualistic aspects of prayer, I still feel this is an act full of love, and so fitting to use within a spiritual context.

Prayers are really a way of asking and communicating in a way that helps us to connect both with our own inner wisdom and also outside of ourselves, whether it is sending love to people around us, to countries far away in times of tragedy, or to a higher place. Prayer is the simplest way that we can talk to heaven; we might ask specific questions in the hope of receiving an answer, or we might ask for protection, comfort or healing. Often we pray for the benefit of others who are in need; we put out our loving and positive feelings towards that person or people.

I think it is easy to get a sense of the power of prayer when we know that we are in someone's prayers – it is a wonderful, uplifting feeling, often just at the moment when we really need something to lift our spirits. Likewise, it feels good to send out our own prayers. We might think of this as like having a conversation with heaven. I'm sure 'they' like to hear from us in this way and I believe that we receive answers to our prayers in many different ways. Sometimes the answer comes clearly in a dream, with the appearance of an earth angel (those mysterious strangers who just seem to appear to help us out), through a friend, a coincidence, sign, or sudden flash of insight. I also think answers are sometimes more subtle, in that prayer has the power to give us courage, heighten our attention, give us hope, ease pain and encourage us to help others.

It appears that prayer may even have the power to heal. There are so many examples of 'miracle' cures that have defied the understanding of modern medicine that many scientists are now investigating the power of the mind and its relationship to the body. Neurologist Dr Antonio Damasio has explored this and talks about how we might cultivate the elemental aspects of our humanity so that we might release our body's 'instinct to heal'. I think that prayer perhaps does just that, not only helping our bodies but also our minds and our hearts. Reaching out has definitely helped me during times of depression, and when I finally allowed myself to feel my grief for the loss of my mother, I in turn allowed myself to ask for and receive help. The way our modern society is set up it is easy to fall into a pattern of isolation in our lives where we can feel achingly lonely; prayer reminds us that we are never completely alone and that we can ask for help – our spiritual guides both in heaven and here on earth will be listening.

I think the following story from Kathleen brings the simple power of prayer to life in a wonderfully uplifting way.

What is it you want?

I was told many years ago by a homeopath that I have a sensitive nature and was bound lifelong to feel everything deeply (good or bad). I didn't want to take this on board at the time, but since then she has been proved right a number of times.

I remember one morning when I was around fifty, I was sitting in the kitchen feeling utterly dejected as my 28-year-old marriage was falling apart and my two sons were all but grown up and soon to have their own lives. Without thinking I just said out loud, 'God help me!' I just couldn't imagine my own future at that point. That's when I heard a voice, strong and kind, say, 'What is it you want?' Well, before I could collect myself and trot out my long list of complaints and needs, my own heart (as I believe it to have been) answered clearly and promptly, 'Peace of mind.'

I was amazed at this sudden clarity. I just knew the holy spirit of God had heard my plea and replied so swiftly. What joy. In short, my life has been so happy in so many ways since, such that I could not have imagined.

Often, spiritual guides will literally shine a light on our life or our thoughts. Kathleen's moment of insight was just the answer she needed in this time of confusion and dejection.

What you know you can't explain but you feel it.
Morpheus, *The Matrix*

In the following story, Brian's prayer is simple and to the point, no need for his heavenly guides to worry about his intention here.

In an instant

My little grandson was two and a half years old, sitting on my wife's knee, sobbing his heart out. He just didn't know what to do with himself. He was feverish, sweating and generally very unwell.

I had just been reading a book about spirits and I thought to myself, 'Come on, Angels, make him better.' At that instant, my grandson jumped off my wife's knee and started laughing and running around, as happy as could be. I was amazed and overjoyed.

Ruby's prayer is less reactive than Brian's in that she foresees that something terrible might happen to her son and his girlfriend in a dream, and so calls for protection when signs begin to appear that her dream might indeed be a premonition.

Dreaming a dream

I dreamt that my son had a white car and was taking his girlfriend out when he had an accident. My husband suspected that something was wrong as we sat having breakfast together the next morning and asked what it was. I relayed the dream to him and we both sent up a prayer for our son's protection.

When our son returned from work that evening he announced that he was borrowing a car from work to take his girlfriend out the next evening. He asked if my husband and I would give him a lift to work in the morning so that he could bring the other car back.

As we drove into the garage where he worked he pointed out the car that he was going to borrow. My husband immediately noticed my reaction as he was very sensitive to this kind of thing. 'Well, was that the car you saw in your dream?' he asked as we left our son at work. I told him that it was and we both sent up another prayer.

As my son left to pick up his girlfriend that evening my heart was in my mouth and as my husband and I would never be able to get to sleep while worrying about him we waited up for his return. To our relief we heard the car pull up outside and in rushed our son asking for a torch, and then running out again with no explanation. On his return a few minutes later he was exasperated and couldn't understand what had happened. He relayed his experience of the evening to us.

The weather was clear and fine when he left home but as he got on the motorway there were fog patches which slowed him down, and then just as the fog cleared and he was about to put his foot down again he noticed the petrol gauge was on empty. It didn't make sense as he had filled up the petrol tank before he left work. However, he thought he should call in at the next petrol station to make sure. It turned out there was plenty of petrol still in the tank – it was almost full – but while checking he noticed that the car had a very soft tyre. He thought he'd better take it easy and drove extra carefully to his girlfriend's house. He was about to change the tyre when he got there, only to discover the tyre was absolutely fine.

They enjoyed their evening, but on leaving for home he noticed again that the tyre was very soft, so he took the return journey steady. On his arrival home he rushed in for the torch, only to find the tyre was completely in order and not soft in the slightest.

A guardian angel helped us out that day.

Helen feels very comfortable with her spirituality, and felt blessed to receive a sign one day while asking for a little bit of help.

Aisha

Hi Theresa, I have been just watching an angel programme on television and it made me think of you. I thought I would write to tell you this little story.

While in meditation I was told I have a new angel, called Anastasia, the 'little princess who was treated cruelly by her own people'. A couple of days after this I remembered and kept hearing her name over and over again, Anastasia. The same thing had happened to me years ago; one name just kept coming into my mind and I thought I must be obsessed with it. Then when I went to see a medium she told me that she could see my angel beside me. She said her name is Isha, that my angel was saying the words, 'I am

Isha.' I said, 'No, that's not right, her name is Aisha.' The medium smiled and said my angel was saying to her, 'Helen knows my name.' Aisha also told me that when she draws near to me my eyes go funny, and it's true my eyes flicker from side to side sometimes. When that happens I always say, 'Hello, Aisha.'

A little while after learning about Anastasia, while on holiday I was getting ready to go to dinner and decided to wear my cross on a chain. It is a very fine chain and it was full of knots; try as I might I couldn't get them out so I said, 'Anastasia, I know you are not really supposed to help but please, please could you take these knots out for me?' Well, Theresa, I picked up the chain to try again and it unravelled right in front of my eyes.

I feel so humble – I never thought I would ever get proof that I had an angel. It brings tears to my eyes and I talk to her often.

I enjoyed reading Jenny's story, which I include here, very much. It's a really good example of how we can call on our celestial guides whenever we need a bit of team support.

A big event

I'm a volunteer community radio presenter and unfortunately a few months ago we lost our premises following a robbery and the loss of our electricity supply. Since then, I've been trying to raise funds to set up a new radio station. Just over three weeks ago, this led to me to realize another of my dreams, which was to set up my own gig and invite my favourite bands to play at it. The gig was the first of my fund-raising efforts and I'm convinced that heaven was watching over the whole thing! Here's my story:

I had been contacting various people, trying to find a suitable venue for my event. For several weeks, I'd been unable to find one, as they were all too expensive, too far away, or unsuitable for my health needs as I suffer from chronic health problems. After a while, I decided to return to a venue I'd been contemplating before. This particular venue is much closer to home and suits all of my needs. It soon became clear to me that this was the venue I felt most comfortable with and in which I'd be able to function best during the event. I arranged a meeting with the owner/manager to discuss the possibility of running the event there. Just prior to attending the meeting, I said a prayer to the angels, during which I asked them to send me a sign if this was the right venue for the event. Just as I was on my way into the venue, something prompted me to look down on the driveway and there, right at my feet, was a white feather. I said thank you to the angels and went into the venue for the meeting. The meeting went amazingly well and turned out even better than I'd expected.

Everything was falling into place and the price for hiring the venue was later confirmed as the cheapest price yet. Still, I wasn't sure how I was going to pay for it, but again I asked the angels to help me to secure the payment some-how and left it in their hands. A few weeks before the event took place, my partner suddenly had some unexpected money come through, which was the exact amount I needed for the hire charge. He kindly gave it to me to allow me to pay for the venue, saying he knew it was one of my dreams.

Prior to securing the payment, several other things had also fallen into place. Everything worked out so that all the bands I wanted were available to play at the event. A new friend came on board to help me organize the Facebook page and by happy synchronicity, his band were the first to agree to play at the event. Being a graphic designer, he also designed the flyers and posters for the event. I had never even met him beforehand, yet I feel that it was definitely a friendship that was meant to be and that the angels guided us to each other at just the right time. We just took to each other as if we'd known each other all our lives. This friend has been an endless source of help and support for me and I honestly believe that it's only down to his input that the event was so well promoted and consequently so successful.

I'd like to add here that considering that it was my first ever big event, it went amazingly well and I've been invited back to do more events in future. Here is what's perhaps the most important part of the story, though. As I mentioned earlier, I have chronic health problems and had been feeling extremely unwell for the previous six months and had barely been able to do anything or even get out of the flat much. Considering how much I wanted this event to work well, I prayed to the angels to allow me to be well enough to be able to cope with and enjoy the day. I'm very happy to say that they answered my prayer and on that day

I felt better and happier than I had in six months. I managed to be completely pain-, fatigue- and illness-free for the whole day. The pain did return, but I was so thankful and I firmly believe and know in my heart that the angels were helping me that day to be able to fulfil my dream and be well enough to see it through. I can honestly say it was one of the happiest healthiest days of my life and not only that, but also I had achieved something I never thought I'd be able to achieve, which was to stand up on the stage and talk to a live audience. Being a radio presenter, who's used to being heard rather than seen, the thought of talking in front of a live audience is something that has filled me with dread all my life and which I never thought I'd be able to do. That day, I achieved it and while I was standing on the stage talking, the fear left me completely. I felt happy, relaxed, comfortable and confident. In fact, I was in my element! It was truly amazing. Whatever anyone may say, I know that it was more than adrenaline that helped me to do that.

Everyone was such a pleasure to work with and it just seems that everyone and everything I needed was sent to me at the right time to enable it to work well for us. We even raised a fair amount of money for a first event. Most of the bands have asked me to invite them to play again at future events and other bands have volunteered too. It really does seem as if this was an event which was meant to be and which the angels were overseeing the whole time. I enjoyed the whole process from start to finish. For me, this has definitely been a testament to allowing my intuition to guide and inspire me.

Zoe's letter reminded me that along with prayer, it is belief that gives us strength and support too, even when we are still raw with grief.

I know he is with me

I lost my fiancé Sean in a motorbike accident in May this year. He was twenty-five, and we were due to be married in August after saving for two years to have the most amazing wedding.

I have always been a strong believer in the afterlife but when I lost Sean I doubted it; it wasn't his time to go and I was so angry he got taken away from me. I hit an all-time low and all I wanted to do was be with him. I was worried about him, wondered what he was doing, if he was okay and then I found your book; I cannot explain well enough in words how it has helped me but it has made me strong enough to carry on. I know Sean is happy and in a wonderful place, more than likely still racing around on his motorbike. I know he is with me and pushing me along and that I can talk to him when I need to. Thank you.

When he shall die,
Take him and cut him out in little stars,
And he will make the face of heaven so fine
That all the world will be in love with night
And pay no worship to the garish sun.

William Shakespeare, *Romeo and Juliet*

Dialling direct

I am always amazed at how adaptable the spirits are when it comes to finding ways to communicate with us, so much so that I have even received stories from people who have had phone calls from heaven. Later in the book I share a wonderful story from a lady who received messages from her departed husband on her Kindle, and here I want to end this chapter with Coralie, who found out about her daughter's abuse by her partner through a mysterious phone call.

Who answered the phone?

My sister and I have always felt that we have connections with angels as we have had many experiences with out-of-the-ordinary happenings; but what I would really like to share with you is the fact that I think my daughter Tanya, who is now thirty-one years old, has her own guardian angel. When she was about two and a half years old I was hanging out the washing in the back garden and Tanya was playing alongside me. My husband came out to tell me he was going to the shops. I was not aware that she had followed him until he came back carrying her, screaming that he had run over her. He said he felt the car lift up so he was certain that the wheel had run over some part of her body. At the hospital she had not a mark on her except for a small cut inside her mouth that could have been from the garden edging. What did he run over or what lifted the car up? We were never able to explain it.

Theresa Cheung

When Tanya was eighteen and was trying to get her licence we were looking for a small automatic car for her but
were having trouble finding one. At this time her grandmother was ill with cancer and passed away. An advertise-
ment appeared in the paper about a week later for a
Datsun. We went to look at it and it was the same colour
and model as her nan's, which she had always loved to bits.
The only difference was this one was an automatic and
Nan's was manual. We are certain that the spirit of her nan
or her guardian angel directed us to this car.

When she was about twenty-one, Tanya moved in with
her boyfriend into a house they purchased together. We
didn't really get on well with her boyfriend but tolerated
him for her sake. Tanya worked with me at the time as a
nurse and we had the same shift so I would pick her up and
drop her off home after work. One morning after our shift,
she invited me in for coffee but as her partner was in a foul
mood I decided not to stay. When I got home I rang to see
if she was okay. The phone was answered but all I heard was
her partner abusing her and calling us all the names under
the sun, telling her where we could go in a very unsavoury
manner. I got into my car and went back to her house, only
to find the front door open but no one around. I went to
her friend's house and found Tanya there very upset; she
told us she no longer wanted to live with her partner. We
had her and her furniture out of the house that afternoon.
We then consulted a lawyer who managed to sort out the
finances enough for her to put down a deposit on a house
of her own.

You might wonder why this is relevant, but you see my daughter insists she did not answer the phone that day – she says it was in her bag on a bench in the house and when she left she just picked up her keys and went without it. Who or what answered the phone to let us know she needed us? We have had many other experiences but these ones we will remember for the rest of our lives.

I hope the stories I have included in this chapter show just how varied our conversations with heaven might be, from moments of intuition and insight that come to us as divine inspiration, to those times when we know more than just chance is on our side and even rare cases of being saved by someone or something that is beyond this world. The power of prayer reminds us that sometimes really all we need to do is talk to our angels, to ask for help or the strength to help others. They may answer with a sign, with a moment of serendipity or the silver lining in a cloudy day, and they will always answer with love.

In the next chapter we will enter into the world of dreams, except that – on occasion, as we will discover, visions in the night are so much more than a dream; they are a chance to connect with heaven. Before we do that I would just like to include Carol's wonderful story that she sent to me about the many ways in which she feels connected with her son Mark.

My heart filled with peace

My daughter gave me one of your books for Christmas and I have been absolutely engrossed in it – there is just so much more to life than we will ever know – and I, personally, have been gifted by my elder son, Mark, who passed twelve years ago.

When Mark's accident happened, like all parents who have lost a child I could not see a way to go on living. My world became a black hole in which I was trapped, and one night I lay in his bed, hugging his pillow, trying in whatever way possible to somehow capture a little part of him. I had sobbed myself into a semi-conscious state when I became aware that there were three men gently stroking and holding my hand; I had the distinct feeling that they were discussing my grief with such concern that I instinctively knew that it was Mark, my father and Mark's paternal grandfather. I don't know how, I just did.

The sensation of a sharp pinprick just under my thumbnail brought me to a state of consciousness; it really hurt and I was confused. I got out of bed and stood under a light so that I could see – there was a pinprick under my thumbnail and when I squeezed my thumb, blood ran down both sides of the nail.

Three days later my son's girlfriend came by, and I showed her the clearly visible pinprick, which had by now darkened into a tiny black dot. As I told her what had happened, she became incredulous, saying, 'Carol, when Mark and I were students working at Woolworths, he always used to tease me by taking the little thumb tacks from the shirt packaging and pretending to prick me with them.'

Inexplicable, but I do know that this event has given me comfort beyond explanation, and carried me through these

last twelve years. I grieve Mark every day, but I am so blessed that he managed to bridge the divide between us, in
such a way that I have no doubt that my son is still with me
and always be, as are all my other loved ones.

This became the first of many divine messages. A few
days later I received a beautiful card from a friend in Ireland
– it had the attached poem in it (see below), and without
these words, together with what happened that night, I do
not think I would ever have survived that period of my life.

Since then, my angels come to me in so many ways:

One Christmas, my granddaughters, who were toddlers
at the time, were all banging away on the piano – it was a
bad day for me as I missed Mark so much. The next day a
note Mark had written me as a little child suddenly appeared. I had forgotten it, but it read, 'I love you, Mum and I
wrote this piece of music for you.' Underneath was a child's
attempt at music writing. So I knew he had been with us
over Christmas.

Another time, in a dream, I walked into Mark in my
pantry. I could feel and smell him, the roughness of his
favourite jersey scratching my cheek. I woke up crying,
but know that night Mark did hug me – I could feel his
love and sadness in the big bear hug, and know that he
misses me too.

Also, I once heard a voice cry 'Stop!' as I was about to
enter an uncontrolled intersection – had I not stopped, a
car that came speeding through would have collided with us
and might have killed both my baby granddaughter and me.

I could write a book of my own, I think, of all the spiritual incidences both my daughter and I have enjoyed, but I would just like to share this final one with you:

When a close family member, Jean, discovered she had cancer three years ago, we spoke frankly and openly about her passing on many occasions. She promised she would find a way to let me know that she was with Mark.

Before her diagnosis, I had started experiencing strange phenomena – a mist which would rise around my feet, or sometimes emanate from my cupboard, like a cloud, and float towards me. It would just fade away when I became aware of it. I only ever told Jean about it, and on one occasion joked with her because the mist had risen around my feet while I was on a loo in Dubai.

After Jean's passing the mist disappeared, but one night came back so strongly that I decided to tell my daughter about it. We contacted the South African Paranormal Society; they visited my home and said that there was certainly nothing threatening here, and in fact it had a serene feeling of happiness about it. They could pick up nothing until we spent some time in my bedroom, where one of them started to speak of a sense of 'over the seas and a strong connection with tea'. They then picked up a strong sense of the military and a male connection coming through as well.

My heart filled with peace: Jean had immigrated to South Africa five years before she passed – like all English people, she loved tea, in fact almost lived on it! The military? My son Mark was a British Royal Marine and had returned from England six months before his accident.

The above incidences are carried in my heart all the time,

and reading your book made me feel truly blessed in having Mark and our Angels guiding me through life. I know that Jean and all our other loved ones are also together, so I have no fear of passing.

Wouldn't it be a wonderful world if the word 'die' was taken out of our dictionary, and replaced by 'passing' instead? Your book goes such a long way towards opening minds and giving people alternatives to think about. I am sorry to have 'bent your ear' with my experiences — it is therapeutic and wonderful to share with a believer, so I may have got a bit carried away!

Here is the poem I was sent when Mark had his accident:

Death is nothing at all,
I have only slipped away into the next room.
I am I, and you are you.
Whatever we were to each other,
That, we still are.

Call me by my old familiar name.
Speak to me in the easy way
Which you always used.
Put no difference in your tone.
Wear no forced air of solemnity or sorrow.

Laugh as we always laughed
At the little jokes we enjoyed together.
Let my name be ever the household word
That it ever was,

Let it be spoken without effect.
Without the trace of a shadow on it.

Life means all that it ever meant.
It is the same as it ever was,
There is absolute unbroken continuity.
Why should I be out of mind
Because I am out of sight?

I am waiting for you.
For an interval.
Somewhere. Very near.
Just around the corner.

All is well.

Henry Scott-Holland

CHAPTER THREE

More than just a dream

She sent the gentle sleep from Heaven, that slid into my soul.

Samuel Taylor Coleridge

A wonderful way to converse with heaven is through our dreams. In dreams spirit can communicate to us in the most direct way, but it is also a gentle way to make contact as we are in a more open state of mind during our sleep. It was through dreams that I first made a connection myself with the spirit world, for which I'm so thankful. The world of our dreams is quite extraordinary; it is a place of infinite possibilities. When we get to know them a little better, our dreams can give us fascinating insights into our own lives, emotions and psyches, allowing our unconscious or our wisdom to give us a helping hand. For me, they are also a very spiritual realm, where sometimes it is easier to see and feel things than during the clear light of day. Through my own experiences and those who have sent me stories over the years I have come to understand that the dreaming mind can bridge the gap between life and what comes next.

Pay attention to your dreams – heaven often speaks directly to our hearts when we are asleep.

Eileen Elias Freeman

Night vision

I've had stacks of letters and emails sent to me from people who believe that they have communicated with a departed love one while they were asleep. They typically refer to this experience as a 'dream' but this is because they don't have any other way of describing it. They will often then add something like, 'but it seemed different from my other dreams', or 'it felt like more than a dream', or 'it was no ordinary dream'. In my writing and my research I like to refer to these experiences as night visions because I have come to believe that there are strong differences between dreams and night visions. Let me explain.

Dreams can be fantastic tools for self-awareness and spiritual growth. They can highlight hidden fears, issues and concerns so they can be resolved in your waking life or pinpoint hidden strength and creativity. I like to think of my dreams as a kind of personal therapist. If you are one of those people who think you don't dream, think again. Everyone, regardless of their age or background, dreams every night and we have hundreds of thousands of dreams over the course of our lives. The reason some people don't think they dream is because if you don't get into the habit of recalling your dreams most of them fade instantly from our memories on waking. However, when dreams are remembered they can offer amazing insights into your psychological development – past, present and future – however illogical or trivial they may seem.

You may not realize it or be able to make sense of it, but every dream you have contains a valuable message from your unconscious. Most of us don't understand this message because it is presented to us in a different language – the language of symbols. There are many books out there to help you interpret dream symbols – and I've written one or two of them myself – but these books are only a guide because what a certain symbol represents for one person will have a different meaning to another. For example, if you dream of a cat and are a cat lover this will be a comforting and reassuring sign but if you are allergic to cats it may have a different meaning altogether.

Symbolic dreams that highlight feelings, hopes and fears and where you need to do some self-analysis to get to the real meaning make up the great majority of dreams, but these are not the kind of dreams I will be discussing in this chapter. A tiny percentage of dreams have a very different feel to them. Whereas symbolic dreams are typically fragmented, incomplete, have an unreal or surreal quality about them and are quickly forgotten on waking, these dreams are well organized, instantly remembered on waking, and they do not fade from a person's memory over time. They can be remembered for months and years after and people who experience them often say that the vision is imprinted forever on their minds and hearts. These dreams also feel lucid and real and the meaning or significance of them is so overwhelmingly clear that taking them literally is the only option. As mentioned above, I don't call these dreams, I call them night visions.

Often when I read accounts of night visions I can't help but notice how similar they are to afterlife experiences that are reported when a person is awake. Accounts like this one sent to me by Kathy:

A great send-off

My father died on 3 August 2007 and I had him cremated because he didn't make his wishes known before he died. Two months ago he came to me in an extraordinary dream and he looked so well and happy. He died from throat and stomach cancer. He told me that he had been very pleased and proud of me for the lovely funeral (his words) I had arranged for him. He said I gave him a great send-off. We had a lovely chat and he looked so well and happy it made me feel happy. He held my hand and then I woke up. People often say you shouldn't take any notice of your dreams but this dream was so different.

Will also told me that there was something very different about the dream he had a few weeks after his father died.

Up and away

A week or so after my father died in 1997 I had this powerful dream. It was no ordinary dream. In my vision my dad
was lying on my bed. Then my dad left his body and smiled
at me. He looked at his earth body and waved his hand as if
to say goodbye, I don't need you now. Then he rose up and
away.

For Jill, a dream visit from her late mother gave her just the
extra impetus she needed to address a health issue that had
been affecting her for many years:

A little help from Mum

Mum died in 1999, aged eighty-three, and I hoped to be
contacted by her in some way but nothing happened until
2002 when I had an amazing dream. In it I was lying in bed
on my back asleep when I became aware of being thumped
on my chest. I awoke to find Mum straddled across my body
beating me as hard as she could. I thought, 'Why is Mum
hitting me like this?', and woke up for real to find that I was
indeed lying on my back and that my heart was pounding
and I couldn't breathe. My nose was blocked and my mouth
shut. In that instant I realized I was in trouble and needed air.
After a few gulps my heart rate calmed down.

Ever since I was a child I had problems breathing through
my nose, but had never had it treated. I knew now that I had

to do something about it and went to see my doctor. This resulted in an operation and since then I've experienced a huge improvement in my breathing.

I had never previously dreamt of Mum and haven't done again since and I can still recall everything vividly ten years later. Perhaps she was alerting me to a dangerous situation?

Brenda took comfort from a 'dream' (she added the inverted commas in her letter, something people will often do as these dreams are different from the everyday) when she felt a message in an amazing scent:

Exquisite scent

When my dear mum Lillian died in 1986 I missed her very much. I thought about her often. One night I had a 'dream'. I was in a very large beautiful room and there was a vase of the most beautiful heavenly flowers with a fragrance much like that of lavender or lilac. The scent was so exquisite. It was a very cool room, such as you'd find in a florist where they keep certain flowers. I sensed it was a gift and the 'message' that I received was that 'Mum is fine' and 'you have no need to worry'.

Allie was also very comforted by a visit from her dad in her dreams.

The most beautiful dream

I lost my dad only four weeks ago. His death was premature at the age of sixty-one, but it was peaceful; I'm twenty-five, so as you can imagine it has hit me pretty hard – it has been hard for all of my family. But my dad has visited me in a dream, and it would give me great comfort if I could share my experience with you and your readers in your future book. I had been asking my dad for days after he passed to come and visit me, to let me know where he is and that most of all he is okay. Well, now I know that he is, because it was the most vivid, clear, beautiful dream I have ever had. It gave me great comfort and the experience has been very restoring to my faith and belief in the afterlife.

Visions of departed loved ones in 'dreams' is something I am often asked about as it does seem to be a fairly common experience. Interestingly, most people don't write to ask me if the experience was real because many are already convinced that it is real – and this is even the case for people who until their experience had no belief in the existence of an afterlife. Following their night vision they are in no doubt that they have been visited by a loved one. This was certainly the case for Sandra, whose story is below.

No need for words

I've also experienced my mum and my dad coming back to me in dreams. I know these visits are a recognized form of

ADC (after-death communication). A short while after my dad died, I dreamed I was walking down a lane near our house, and Dad was there waiting for me. He was wearing his favourite old cardigan, and he was beaming all over his face. He looked so well. He hugged me and although he didn't say anything, I knew he was happy and alright.

Three years ago, my mum died – she was eighty-six. She'd been fit and well right up to her unexpected death of pneumonia, and she still went to the supermarket each week, insisting on carrying a couple of bags of shopping home (I lived with my mum up till her death). When she got home, she used to knock on the front door, rather than struggle to put the bags down and find her key.

A short while after she died, I dreamed that I was in the kitchen and the house was filled with a translucent white light. I suddenly heard the familiar knock on the door, and, going to open it, found Mum on the doorstep, laughing. She came in and we hugged and cried, but they were tears of joy. It seemed so natural and right. Again, there was no need for words.

And it is also the case for Georgina:

Last night

Last night in my dream I met my dear grandmother for the first time since her death in November last year. It was at the end of a sad, disturbing dream when I needed some comfort. I saw a huge wooden door slightly ajar and opened it to find myself in the most beautiful room I have ever seen, sort of like a chapel. It was filled with trinkets and other objects I have never seen before. I accidentally knocked some over, but it didn't matter. To my delight, my grandmother Eileen was sitting straight ahead of me watching TV! She looked about sixty-five and she turned off the TV and smiled at me. I asked her if she would like to go somewhere else and she told me she was happy. I was so pleased to see her, I ran over and hugged her tightly. I could smell her perfume and told her how much I missed her. She said, 'I miss you too.' I started to cry and woke up sobbing. I truly believe I was holding her.

She was ninety-six when she died and the last few years she wasn't herself at all. She barely recognized anyone and in the last few months she couldn't eat, so faded away to skin and bone. It was very sad to see. I was very close to my gran as a child and I feel that I will now be able to go back into that chapel room to see my gran again should I wish to.

This 'dream' wasn't the usual jumble of things you've done in the day and seen on TV. It was a perfectly clear, lucid experience. I've no doubt at all that I really met with my beloved grandmother.

And here is what happened to Mary:

Pop's smile

My pop died seven years ago from cancer, and although he was sick and we knew he was dying, when the time came I was absolutely inconsolable. I am his oldest grandchild and loved growing up around him – he just had this way about him that made you feel like you were the most important thing in the world, and though he did this with all his grand-children and family it still felt amazingly special to every one of us. Anyway, I was grieving so strongly but at the same time was trying to tell myself it was totally irrational to be so upset. One night after a bad day I went to bed and took a while to get to sleep. Then I had the most amazing experi-ence I've ever had – so real, so incredible. I dreamt I was at my parents' house and felt the need to get up and open the curtains. When I did, my pop was sitting cross-legged but floating outside the window. The amazing light and warmth were incredible; he was watching me with the most beauti-ful smile and I felt this amazing feeling of love. He didn't speak but I felt him tell me he was okay now and that he loved me very much. It was the most surreal and unique experience I've ever had. The next morning I felt so loved and although I was still grieving my sadness had subsided somewhat so I could control it. I still miss him so much now but I always think about that night and know he's there.

Laureen had a similar experience with a grandparent:

Chatting with Nana

My great-nana died when I was five years old. At the time I wasn't too upset because I was so young and didn't under-stand. About a week after she died, I started having the same dream every night that my nana would fly through my bedroom window, sit on the end of my bed and we would talk for hours. Sometimes I would write notes for her and leave them on my desk for when she came. About six months later it was my sixth birthday and I had a party at a local soft play centre. I remember standing looking at all the parents and right in the middle of them my nana was sitting there waving at me and saying happy birthday. I will always remember the experience and I feel her way of contacting me was through my dreams as I was so young. Still now if I ever feel down I will think about the dreams and it always cheers me up, I believe in angels and I know my great-nana is one.

Many psychologists, therapists and doctors I have spoken to argue that such experiences are simply the product of the grieving mind searching for relief from the pain of loss. I have some sympathy for this argument but the more I have studied the phenomenon the more I have come to believe that it cannot be dismissed so casually. All the stories I have received are evidence for me that night visions are indeed messages of love and reassurance from those who have crossed over.

I have heard and read many stories of loved ones returning to offer support and guidance when it is needed the most. For Kelly, this support helped her through a very sad and traumatic time:

Theresa Cheung

My boys

I've always believed in angels, but have never believed as much as I do now, so here goes. In February 2011, I discovered I was pregnant for the very first time and was absolutely delighted as I had tried for around three years previously to conceive. I couldn't contain my excitement as the pregnancy developed, and when I felt the first tiny kick, the joy was elevated. That was until one awful day in July when I discovered at twenty-six weeks via a scan that my baby boy had tragically died.

From that day on my confidence was crushed and dreams were dashed. Nearly a year later, I again discovered I was pregnant. So much fear came over me and I really couldn't enjoy this second pregnancy as much as I wanted to. I was terrified it would happen again. My instincts were right and I miscarried at sixteen weeks.

Shortly after losing my second child, I had a very comforting dream. I had spent every night since wondering if my boys were okay and free from suffering. My dream came to me as a very bright white sheet of light, and three figures appeared. One adult and two children. I could not see their faces, but believe them to be my nan, who I prayed would look after my sons, and my two boys. The adult took the hands of the children as they grew their wings before my eyes and walked away. I believe this was my sign and my prayer heard.

Since my sixteen-week miscarriage I also suffered another two losses, both at five weeks. The pain and feelings of loneliness became too much for me to bear, and subsequently I took myself to a nearby bridge. I climbed the barrier and although I was ready to jump, I heard a voice telling me I'm not ready and have unfinished business. This made me climb back over the barrier to safety.

Just as I climbed back over, my phone rang. It was my mum. She never calls me out of the blue but had called to ask me if I was alright, because she had an eerie feeling something was wrong. Of course I lied as I didn't want her to panic, but she has since found out about it.

Since then I have learned to adapt to my losses and have not given up hope of having a rainbow child, as I and so many people call them, and have found so many more feathers than ever before. Even clouds make me smile.

For Joy, dream visits from her departed husband gave her simple but profound comfort and the chance to say how much she loved him:

Fred

Since the passing of my dear husband, Fred, I have these 'dreams' of him regularly. The first night he came there was another being or spirit there too and so I felt unnerved when my husband tried to pull back the bedclothes, wanting to get in. The next time, however, there was no other being, just my husband, and so when he got into the bed and snuggled down I welcomed him and I said to him, feeling pleased,

'There, I told you there was more.' In this life, he did not have the same beliefs as I had. Knowing he always had cold feet, I touched his foot with mine and felt it was warm. 'That's alright then,' I said.

Another time, when he put his arms around me in my 'dream', I told him how much I missed him and he held me closer, never speaking. It seemed so real. I told him I was sorry if I had ever taken him for granted, because in this life he had been a wonderful husband, father, grandfather and great-granddad. I could go on and on, but I wanted to share a few of my 'dreams' with you.

Heather consciously opened her mind to the possibilities of dreaming and was able to experience contact with her husband who had passed:

The dreaming self

I have just finished reading your book *Celtic Angels*. I was struck by your account of your battle with depression. Almost from the moment I started reading the book my tears dried, I started to smile and I felt a sense of comfort until late last night when I finished it. I then thought about whether to write to you.

Two nights ago I was about halfway through your book and before I went to sleep I remembered the phrase 'the dreaming self'. I then fell asleep and had a lovely dream in which I encountered my dead husband. All the emotions were still there between us, as they had been in our life together. I even reminded him that he was dead, but it didn't matter because at that moment we were on the same plane together. When I awoke it felt as though we had again shared time together, as we had when he was alive.

One of the reasons why departed loved ones may choose to connect with us in this way is that when we are asleep our unconscious is more receptive to receiving messages from the other side. However, from the stories I have read it seems that although night visions often happen when a person is in a state of deep sleep they can also happen when a person is neither fully asleep nor awake but in that halfway twilight stage. During this twilight stage the body is still half asleep but the brain is alert and night visions are often experienced then. From my own experiences I know that I am more likely to have creative insights or psychic experiences when I am just about to fall asleep or just about to wake up. This may explain why many of the people who write to me say things like, 'I was lying down and feeling tired but I know I didn't dream it.' Or 'I was awake and asleep at the same time,' or 'I know I wasn't dreaming.' There are a number of ways to consciously enter this drowsy state – for example, through meditation, contemplation, hypnosis or deep relaxation – but it can also happen unconsciously and spontaneously through day-dreaming or, as mentioned above, in that twilight drowsy state when we are drifting off to sleep or waking up. From the research I have done, afterlife encounters tend to happen either during times of trauma or during times when a person feels extremely relaxed and many night visions certainly fall into the latter category.

Since they tend to occur when we are fast asleep or in a state of deep relaxation, night visions may also be one of the best ways for loved ones to visit and reassure us without causing unnecessary alarm, especially for those like me who have a nervous disposition. After my mother died I begged for her to make contact with me but the medium she wisely chose was through my dreams. I longed for something more concrete but with hindsight I can now understand that I wasn't ready for anything else. I had too much self-doubt and fear and this would have closed my mind and my eyes to anything else.

I talked earlier about my own experience of a night vision on the night I narrowly escaped death in a car accident, but it is not only because I have experienced them myself that I'm convinced that night visions are indeed messages of hope and love from the other side. Reading countless stories from ordinary people with true hearts, like this vivid and memorable account sent to me by Michelle, has also convinced me.

Time of my life

Eleven years ago after a long battle with osteoporosis my mother died. My sister and I spent a long two years caring for her and when she passed away my sister suggested that as soon as the funeral was over we both go on a very long holiday to give ourselves time to grieve and also time to plan ahead for the future. I wasn't married at the time and there was nothing to hold me back so we booked ourselves on a flight to Australia and planned to spend two months there. Yet about a week before we were due to fly out I lost my nerve. I felt it was wrong to be backpacking around the world like we were a couple of teenagers and that it was wrong to be enjoying ourselves so soon after our mother had died.

I was becoming really negative about the trip and was about to tell my sister I couldn't go through with it when I had this brilliant dream. In it my mum appeared and sat down on the bed beside me. She looked wonderful. Her skin and her hair were glowing and her posture was perfect. Before she died her bones had got so weak she was almost bent double. She brushed my fringe away from face – the way she always used to do when I was a child – and said, 'Pull yourself together now. I don't want you to put your life on hold because of me. If you don't go on this trip now life will flash by and you'll never have seen much of the world. Enjoy your life as much as you can. I'll let you in on a secret: I'm having the time of my life over here,' and then she laughed and vanished. Her high-pitched chuckle was so unmistakably the laugh of my mum that I could not question the dream.

I told my sister the next day how excited I was about the trip and how I was determined to soak up every moment. And enjoy it I did. I had the time of my life. It was just the tonic I needed after the past few years of struggling and grief. My sister didn't believe me when I told her but all these years later I remain convinced that this dream wasn't like any other dream I have had and that my mother did visit me in the night.

If you still feel confused at this stage about the difference between dreams and night visions I hope the following information will prove useful to you. Over the years that I have been reading stories about night visions I have been able to distinguish a number of clear characteristics that set them apart from symbolic dreams. First and foremost, on waking a person will instantly recall their experience. It will be a vivid image in their minds, unlike symbolic dreams which are not always easy to recall. Second, the night vision will not fade from memory in minutes as symbolic dreams do. The dreamer will often be able to remember their dream in detail not just minutes or hours later but many months and years later. Third, the overwhelming majority of night visions tend to take place in a setting that is realistic and familiar, most typically the bedroom of the dreamer. A person may be lying down just about to go to sleep and then they will see a vision of a loved one. This in itself is fairly unusual as most dreams do not have the bedroom as their setting. Fourth, there will be no story or plot or even action in the vision. It will simply involve the loved one appearing and communicating in some way. Again this is unusual, as most dreams have a great deal of plot, action and confusion. (Having said this, I have also had stories about loved ones interrupting a dream. Suddenly, the dream will change from a surreal or confused setting to a realistic and familiar setting.) Fifth, the loved one in the vision will appear in such a realistic and convincing way that the person will have absolutely no doubt they have appeared to them in spirit. Also, both during and after the experience the person will be entirely convinced that was is happening is real and not imagined. They sense the closeness of their loved one and on waking that sensation remains. Again this is entirely different from symbolic dreams of loved ones or people you know. On waking you know you dreamed about these people and didn't actually meet them.

Dreams about those who have died are a recognized part of the grieving process but there is a difference between symbolic dreams and night visions, which have the characteristics mentioned above. I truly believe that night visions are a form of afterlife communication and so do all the people who have written to me about their experience of them. Many of these people also say that their night vision was a source of great comfort and they notice within themselves an immediate and significant change. Their grief does not disappear, it is just somehow easier to cope with.

For Ana Rita, it was through a night vision that her grandmother could tell her everything was going to be okay:

Inner peace

When I was twelve my parents got divorced. One night my father came to my room to tell me that they didn't want any judge to decide which one I should stay with; only I could decide that, and they would always be there for me no matter what. He started to cry – it was the first time I saw my father crying and I forgot my sadness and tried to comfort him. I told him that I would stay with my mother but I would be with him all the time. It was so hard to say this and we cried together.

Then in December 2005 we got a phone call from a

cousin, saying that my grandmother (my father's mother) was very weak. She was a brilliant granny, always playing and joking. By then I was the only grandchild in the family with a degree and she was so proud of it. My mother called her to arrange dropping off her Christmas presents the next day. I could hear my grandma on the line but her voice was so fragile I started to cry, because I knew what was going to happen and I could sense Granny trying not to say she wouldn't be there in the morning. She passed away that night. I was devastated; she was the first person who was very close to me who I had lost.

The next day I remember parking the car in front of the church and there was my father crying for the second time in my life. He opened his arms to me and hugged me in such a way that even today when I want to remember him I remember that hug. It was strong, emotional, warm, heartfelt, genuine – it was perfect.

A few months passed, then one night my grandma came to me in my dreams. She looked younger and never opened her mouth. We talked telepathically and she said everything was alright. After this dream I accepted she was gone and got back my inner peace somehow. She brought me love, peace, and the energy to keep going.

In the case of violent or sudden or unexpected death, the grief of many people is doubled by wondering about how much a person may have suffered before their death. Again night visions offer reassurance. This next story from Tatiane illustrates this well.

The message of forgiveness

In 2011 my brother Elon died in a car accident – he was just twenty-three. He was my only brother, and there were ten years between us so I almost took care of him like a son, always fussing too much and loving too much. The suffering I felt when he died was immense, crazy and destructive.

After many sleepless nights, many doubts, many questions, and too many dreams, one dream in particular caught my attention. In the dream, which felt almost real, I heard my brother in his room, watching TV and laughing loudly. I looked at my mother and said Elon is here (in the dream we knew he had died). I went to his room, and he was lying in bed watching TV as usual. He talked to me, asking if I had found him handsome in the movie that he had done, *Mary Magdalene*. Suddenly I woke up, but with the image of the dream in my head, the words he spoke, all too real. I talked to my mother, told her the dream, and asked if she knew of a movie with this title, but she hadn't heard of it. I searched the internet and found the film *Mary Magdalene*, which I watched a few days later with my mother. I felt my brother had mentioned the movie to give me a message. I believe he wanted me to forgive the boy who was driving in the accident, who had drunk too much and flipped over the car (my brother was the only one who died – he had been hitchhiking). The message of forgiveness in the film is very strong, and that helped us a lot to not keep a grudge against the driver, and believe that yes there is life after death, and that our deceased loved ones use dreams to send us messages.

I have always believed that my guardian angel watches over me, and has helped me out of tricky situations, and protects me from the unforeseen.

For me, the comfort and reassurance that a night vision brings is perhaps the most significant piece of evidence yet. If the experience was imaginary how could it create such an immediate and positive change? In addition, when people are grieving their minds and hearts are filled with intense pain, confusion, anger and upset, and to have a comforting dream reassuring them that life is eternal emerging from this state of anxiety is highly unusual. It is far more likely in my opinion for a night vision to have emerged from a heavenly rather than a human source, but that, as I said, is my opinion. At the end of the day it is your decision that matters.

As you should know by now I believe that dreams can easily connect us with loved ones who have passed away, but not only do I think they can bridge the gap between this life and the next, I also believe that they can bridge the gap between time and space, past, present and future.

Here is Beverley's fascinating account.

Dream premonition

I've just read your wonderful book *An Angel Changed My Life*. I'm not even sure why I selected it at the library but the remarkable stories and your commentary have gone some way to answering my questions about an experience I had that has, in equal measures, baffled and comforted me.

I'm not sure where my story lies in the spectrum of supernatural experiences but I would like to share it with you.

On 1 September last year I woke up just before my alarm and was aware of movement at the bottom of my bed – it didn't take shape or form but was more like a fleeting dark blue heat haze. I remember blinking and trying to focus and then I heard my mum's voice very clearly saying, 'I won't appear to you because that'll freak you out but I'll come to you in your dreams.'

I must say that it left me feeling very anxious because it was so real I was convinced Mum must have passed away. I set off for work and at the earliest opportunity phoned Mum 'just to check'. To my relief she was her normal, cheerful self but for the next couple of weeks I felt dogged by a feeling of dread. Mum and I were really close and talked every day and she was in fine fettle so there was no reason to feel like this.

On 13 September I phoned Mum as usual and there was no answer. I immediately knew something was wrong and asked my uncle to check on her. Sadly my mum had suffered a heart attack and passed away. The family gathered and I returned home next day in shock and in bits. And this is where lovely coincidences started happening ... I switched on the TV – more for a distraction than anything else as I was too numb to process anything – and the first thing I heard was a quiz show host asking a question about Pocahontas. I laughed and cried at the same time (probably hysteria!) because Mum and I had a standing joke about her being related to Pocahontas. A week or so later when I was feeling full of despair I also saw a rainbow. Just little things like that lifted my spirits.

About four weeks after Mum's passing I was still utterly bereft and needing to hear that she was okay. I didn't know what to do and for some reason decided to phone a medium/clairvoyant. Although I admit to having a strong belief in such things, I'm not convinced by these 'dial a psychic' lines – they seem to focus on love lives and meeting Mr Right. However, the 'reader' without prompting started talking about my mum and told me she was with her and said, 'She says that she's well and her knees are okay – she won't appear to you because that will freak you out but she will come to you in your dreams, true love never dies' … coincidence? I don't think so – they are the exact words that were said to me when I awoke that morning. I know my mum is okay and she is looking after me.

So there you go. Did I have a premonition … was it a message? I don't know – but I feel so humbled and comforted by this experience. I've also revised my thoughts about phone psychics :-).

Beverley's story is intriguing and when I read it I was reminded of the strange and wonderful way the dreaming mind can work and the stunning proof I feel it offers that we are all spiritual beings with the ability to communicate across physical boundaries of space and time. Mandi's story is similar in that she believes she was also given a warning.

Watching from above

When I was nine my grandfather was dying of cancer but at the time I didn't know that because my family didn't want to worry me. They just told me he was feeling poorly. One night I dreamt he had died. In my dream I saw who was with him when he died and where everyone was in the house at the time and what they were doing. It was as if someone had taken the roof off the house and was watching from above. I heard my aunt say, 'He's gone' and then I woke up.

I asked my mum if Granddad was okay and she told me had had a good night and had slept well. I felt horrible that I had dreamed of him dying and didn't say anything about my dream. The next night my mum and dad went to help with my granddad as they had done for weeks now and I was allowed to stay up late to watch TV with my older sisters. My aunt came in a few hours later and I don't know why but I just looked at her and told her my granddad had died. I felt very peaceful and calm, even though I loved my granddad very much. My aunt asked me if Mum had phoned and my sister said she hadn't. My sisters got very upset and didn't ask me anything else.

I never mentioned my dream to anyone until years later when my aunt and mum were discussing Granddad's death. They asked me how I had known and I told them about my dream. They could not believe it because it happened exactly as I had dreamed it. My dream felt like my granddad was showing me what was going to happen so I would know that he was okay and wasn't suffering or afraid any more.

Debra wrote to me and described her feelings of despair when her beloved husband died suddenly and how a dream experience gave her a feeling of hope, comfort and calm.

An angel spoke to me

I have just read your book *An Angel Spoke to Me*. And I feel moved enough to send an email.

My husband passed away suddenly aged forty. We had just returned from a lovely two-week holiday, he became ill at the end and we didn't think much of it but four days after our return he died. He was diagnosed with Acute promyelocytic leukaemia and died just hours later.

Since then I have apparently been 'very brave' 'inspirational,' and many, many more words I can't really believe. However, twice during this time of grief I have been caught in the very bottom of the worst despair and something has happened to me to stop me and help me climb up the ladder again.

The first time I was sobbing so hard I could not breathe, but my over-riding thought was that I could understand why some people could hurt themselves to stop the pain, and I felt close to cutting myself; I was about to go and get a knife. I have never ever wanted to do anything like that before and I don't know why now other than the loss of my husband was so deep. But something stopped me – I don't know what how or why but something made me turn on my computer and find the number for the Samaritans. I didn't actually call them. It took me quite a long time but eventually I was able to slow my crying and control my breathing and eventually fell onto the bed and slept for several hours. I can't remember anything else about my feelings that night but I remember feeling calm as I dropped off to sleep.

The second time was a few weeks ago. Again I got into a low state similar to before, but not too hurt myself. I was in bed and again sobbing uncontrollably; this time however I called out loudly several times to my husband, telling him I wished he could come back to me because I needed him here with me. Then I felt an impulse to look to the corner of the room; I can only say that I felt like there was a shadow in the corner, and that it never moved. I kept checking and telling myself I was being silly but at the same time I also was slowing my crying and breathing better, then as I started to drift asleep I felt like I was being enveloped as though by strong arms, just as if it was my husband, and again I fell asleep in a deep and comforting sleep.

I told my good friend about this second incident and she got up, gave me your book and told me I was ready to read it now.

I honestly do not know what I think about these two episodes and what the outcome could mean, but after reading your book I guess it's possible that in my sleep I had a visitation by my guardian angel, or my husband.

I have always been a little middle of the road in my belief,

I still don't know one way or the other but if it helps me grieve and continue my journey then I am happy to see where it takes me. The odd part is my husband definitely did not believe so if he did come to me, well, it would be so far away from his core but that he would do it for me if he thought it would help me.

Thank you for writing the book and for letting it find its way to my friend so she could help me.

Yvonne also had a dream vision into the future, which was related to her husband.

Dreaming of a yellow tank

When I married I went to live in Germany as my husband was in the Army. I remember one night I had a vivid dream that felt very real. I could see my husband in an Army tank and it was painted yellow, not the normal colour of a tank, and this tank was rolling across desert sand. I woke up suddenly and cried out to my husband, 'Wake up! Wake up! You're going to a desert.' He told me not to be silly and go back to sleep.

Six months later he was deployed to the first Gulf War. I think I prayed every day without fail for him to return safely, which I'm glad to say he did.

For Hazel, it was through a dream or night vision that she received a warning that saved her family:

An urge to check downstairs

When I was married, my husband and I slept in the attic and our son and daughter slept on the floor below us. On this night, they were about four and five years of age. I had had an early night and by the time my husband came to bed I was fast asleep. It was in the early hours that I woke up and felt unsettled. I wasn't in pain but it wasn't a nice feeling – I felt very disturbed about something. Every time I began to doze off, I woke up again, as though I was being made to stay awake. I went down the attic stairs to where the children were sleeping, and then carried on downstairs towards the kitchen. I'm terrified of the dark but for some reason I didn't turn on the lights, and as I reached the bottom of the stairs I could smell something strong and horrible. I suddenly realized it was gas and as I opened the kitchen door I heard the cooker hissing as gas was pouring out. My husband had moved his lunch bag before going to bed and managed to get the strap wrapped around one of the knobs, so inadvertently turning on the gas.

I have often wondered if it was just a coincidence that I kept waking up that night, why I felt like someone was not allowing me to sleep. I also wonder why I never turned on the lights downstairs, even though I am so scared of the dark. If I had flicked the switch who knows what could have happened with all that gas that had leaked from the cooker. I would love to know if this was the work of my or my children's guardian angel. I'll never know, but I suspect someone was looking out for us that night.

You may notice the relief many of those who send stories to me mention at being able to share it with someone who isn't going to ridicule or laugh at them. This relief is a familiar theme for many people who write to me about afterlife experiences. In each case I write back to tell these people how proud I am of them and how much difference they are making by writing to me and allowing me to share their stories because I know how much their accounts and experiences can bring comfort to others.

If you ever have a vivid and realistic dream like some of those mentioned in this chapter or indeed an experience like those mentioned in this book I urge you to write it down and share it with as many people as possible. If you feel that you won't be taken seriously, start by saying something unusual but amazing happened to you, or if you really don't feel comfortable, send your story to me. You have no idea what a difference you can make in this way.

I hope what you have read so far will have shown you that night visions are different from symbolic dreams and that they can provide as much comfort and reassurance as afterlife encounters that happen when a person is awake.

Out-of-body experiences

Another category of afterlife encounter which belongs in this chapter because it typically happens when a person isn't fully conscious is the out-of-body experience. There are many accounts from people who state they have encountered a departed loved one during an out-of-body experience or OBE.

In my mind, OBEs – when a person temporarily leaves their body to travel in spirit form – offer yet more convincing evidence that there is more to us than our physical bodies. Some argue that the experience is nothing more than a dream, but to anyone who has had the experience – and from my research I know there are thousands of you – it is so much more than a dream. It is a vivid spiritual reality.

OBEs have been reported for centuries. During an OBE a person leaves their physical body and travels in spirit form to other places on earth or other spiritual dimensions. Many people who have had a near-death experience or NDE claim to have had an OBE but the difference between OBE and NDE is that you do not need to be close to death to experience an OBE. Typically it happens when people are asleep or lying down or deeply relaxed.

For Danielle, an OBE experience in childhood gave her a yearning for a more spiritual way of life.

Rising up

I used to experience the sensation of rising up to the ceiling – this only ever occurred in the lounge of the house in which I grew up. The memories of these happenings feel very real, in that I don't ever remember them as dreams. Even as I write this, I can remember the sensation of rising up. These sensations occurred when I was alone and had not been in bed. Or had I been in bed and the dream so vivid as to make it feel like it happened during waking moments?

I also used to feel myself float out of bed, down the stairs to the front door. However, on these occasions I did feel a little unnerved and wanted urgently to be back in bed. I would feel my body land back in bed, although I don't ever recall seeing my body in bed as I floated back towards the bed. One night four years ago my good friend passed over after taking his own life. Around midnight I felt someone standing by my bed, and as I turned over, I saw a shadow that disappeared. It was only after talking to his family that I realized that this was the time that he had left his home to carry out his actions. Could this have been a visitation? These occasions have always intrigued me, and as my yearning for a deeper, more spiritual way of life has deepened, my mind is full of questions. My wonderful Nan passed over five years ago and I long to feel her around me and make contact. I do talk to her every day, and light a candle by her photo at night.

In the following story, one reader described a sensation of 'being up on the ceiling' looking down on the situation unfolding below. It was as though she needed to be able to leave her body to gain perspective and then she knew exactly what she needed to do to get herself out of a tricky and potentially very dangerous situation.

Up on the ceiling

A few years ago, I qualified as a massage therapist and aroma-therapist. I was building up my client base, but was still quite inexperienced. And I broke a Golden Rule. Namely … do not see unknown male clients in your own home when there is no one there with you. My client, who I will call Johnny, weighed about twenty stone, and arrived wearing a bright green woolly hat. He had come for a deep-tissue treatment that he felt might help a hamstring injury. It became apparent during the session that all was not well with Johnny's mental health. I can only think that his medication (which he had made no mention of during consultation) must have worn off, and to cut a very long story short, after I had called 999, I found myself wedged between a sofa and a sideboard in front of a window, being confronted by a now naked and very upset Johnny. The next thing I knew, I was up on the ceiling looking down at the scene. I can clearly remember feeling incredibly light and happy, and not at all concerned about my dire situation. In fact I was giggling to myself, thinking, 'If they could only see me now' (meaning if only my friends could see the ridiculous situation I had got myself into).

At that moment, I was suddenly back in my body again, and I seemed to know exactly what to do, as if I had been given clear instructions. I turned around and opened the window to call down to a non-existent neighbour, asking her if she could please come upstairs for a moment. This stopped Johnny in his tracks, and I knew that I had to keep calm and encourage him to please put on his clothes before my neighbour or the police arrived. The police did arrive and removed a now just sockless Johnny from my home.

I was left thanking my Guardian Angel profusely, promising never to put myself in that situation again!

Angela's son Max had this dream when he was just five years old:

The stars are our home

Max said to me: 'I had a dream, Mummy, that we were at Aunt Julie's and you and I and Grandma Sofie jumped off a cliff into the water (not deep water) then we had wings that took us up to the stars. The stars are our home, Mummy, we go to live in the stars.' He named everyone who was there – my sisters, their husbands and children – all the most important people to Max in his life.

I was amazed by his dream and asked, 'What colour were our wings, darling?' and he replied, 'They were blue and rainbow-coloured. Our wings took us up to the stars.'

In all the accounts of OBEs I have read, the same words – 'it felt so real' – keep coming up. It seems that in spirit, things feel more complete and more vivid than in everyday life. Communication with departed loved ones also seems to take place by telepathy.

Like night visions, many people who have had an OBE describe it as a dream but that is simply because they have no other word to describe it or haven't done research on OBEs. Fortunately, though, there has been a great deal of investigation into the phenomenon and this research shows that the experience is far more common than you might think. It also shows that you don't need to be close to death to have an OBE and that everyone who experiences it feels that it is more than just a dream. It is my hope that further studies of these experiences will provide even more proof that there really is life after death.

Sleep working

Many different names have been given to the part of us that survives death and can travel outside the body and these include soul, astral body, heavenly body and – my favourite – spirit. And while we are on the subject of spirit travelling outside the body, I want to close this chapter by mentioning perhaps my favourite category of night-time adventures. These are experiences in which people find their spirit bodies leaving their physical bodies during sleep to undertake the important spiritual work of helping dying people cross over to the other side. Again a hallmark of these experiences is that they feel incredibly vivid and real.

People who have these experiences say that when they fall asleep they often find themselves leaving their bodies to help the dying. Janet sent me this story and I'm including it here because it is a great example of what I am talking about.

A hand to hold

One night I had a dream in which a lady came to me and conveyed (she spoke through her mind, not verbally) that she was dying and would I hold her hand while she passed over? I conveyed that I would, and then she indicated that she was leaving someone behind and she didn't know how he would cope, and would I be there for him? Again, I agreed, puzzled as to who these people were. After this I had a distinct feeling of floating up to the ceiling, in a strange room, still holding the woman's hand. Suddenly the room was filled with a brilliant light and I knew she had passed over. The dream ended there.

This may sound like a sad dream but it wasn't – far from it – there was a beautiful, almost joyous feeling about it, and the light was amazing and loving.

For Valerie, it was an acquaintance who told her she had visited her in her dreams and helped out in a time of need:

Herbal healer

I am very interested in herbs and their healing properties and have studied them for many years. I belonged at one time to a Herb Club where like-minded women got together once a month to share our love for them.

One day one of the members (I didn't know her particularly well) came up to me during the tea break to tell me about something that had happened to her. She'd apparently been very ill with bronchial pneumonia and was battling for air when she said, 'You and your angels came to lift me up to help me breathe.' She insisted it hadn't been a dream. I had no recollection of the incident myself, but wonder if I could have been with her while I slept?

Ruby was just twelve years old when she was transported in her dreams to be a companion to her aunt's friend Jean as she passed over. It is a beautiful story, I think.

A companion for Jean

I have had what I now know as precognitive dreams since I was four years of age. These dreams are so real that they are never erased from our minds; they seem to stay with us all of our lives.

I was twelve years old and had just started my new school a few weeks earlier. Instead of staying in school for lunch I used to go to my auntie's, who lived and worked in the same town. On occasions a friend of hers who she worked with would come for lunch too. I remember Jean was a very beautiful and very nice woman. But I hadn't seen my aunt's friend for a few days, and in those days children were seen and not heard so I was not aware why she hadn't been for lunch.

In the early hours of the morning I had this dream. I found myself 'swimming' up a steep bank of luscious, long, green silky grass with Jean just ahead of me and calling out that it was very hard to swim up here. As we reached the top of the hill there was a large stone-built mansion ahead of us. We crossed the road and entered by a large oak door much like a church door, with iron studs in it. There was a passageway and a large hall laid with flagstones housing a large medieval table with five place settings. At the far end of the room was a large stone fireplace with a lovely warm fire burning brightly.

Jean turned her back to the fire and held her skirts up to warm herself, just like she did at my aunt's home. Then I followed her as she walked back towards the hall and started to mount a beautiful staircase, the type we see in grand medieval homes belonging to the wealthy. As she got to the top I started to follow her but as I approached about the third stair a bright white light shone out and drove me back to the bottom of the staircase. I tried three more times to go up the stairs but the light kept driving me back down. I woke up unable to see, still blinded by the light from my dream. I called out to my mum, who came to calm me down and make me a cup of tea as I told her my dream.

I remember it was a Sunday and as usual that day Mum was rushing around getting the Sunday lunch ready, after which she made a quick exit to go and visit my aunt for the afternoon. It was some time later that I learned she had gone to see how Jean was as she had been taken to the hospital a few days earlier with what turned out to be an inoperable brain tumour. Jean had passed away during the night.

When I first started getting stories about these kinds of experiences twenty years ago I was convinced they were nothing more than dreams, but over the years I have heard a number of accounts and as with night visions and out-of-body experiences I am now convinced they are real experiences. I don't have any clear memories of doing spiritual work in my sleep but if the dreaming mind can connect us with the afterlife there is a very strong possibility that many of us are drawn to spiritual work in our sleep.

Perhaps you have woken up after a good eight-hour sleep feeling exhausted? If there aren't any medical reasons for this and you can't figure out any other possible explanation for your tiredness, why not consider the possibility that your spirit has had a very busy night? Perhaps you were there offering comfort and guidance to someone who passed over. It is a wonderful thought that when we fall asleep we may all wake up to our spiritual reality.

We all live such busy lives today and many of us don't give our sleeping hours a second thought but, as this chapter has shown, when we are asleep or drifting in and out of sleep the barriers of logic and scepticism disappear and our spirits can soar. And perhaps one day, as more studies are done, meeting a loved one in your dreams won't be dismissed as wishful thinking or imagination or 'just a dream' but recognized as the wonderful, comforting and deeply spiritual experience that it truly is.

Have you ever had a dream, Neo, that you were so sure was real? What if you were unable to walk from that dream, Neo? How would you know the difference between the dream world and the real world?

Morpheus, *The Matrix*

CHAPTER FOUR

Spirit calling cards

I swear to you there are divine things more beautiful than words can tell.

Walt Whitman

Signs are designed to help us find our way, whether driving along a road, walking along the coast path or even when it comes to matters beyond the physical realm. One of the most common but extraordinary ways heaven can speak to us is through signs, or 'spirit calling cards', such as feathers, coins, rainbows, clouds and objects moving mysteriously.

Signs like these help us to understand, accept and even embrace the idea that death is not really the end, but rather a whole new beginning. For me, the sign that helped me so much to release some very deep hurts and resentments related to my grief was seeing the perfect image of an angel in a cloud on a blue-sky day.

I think that heaven's calling cards are like any greeting card, offered with a message of love. Sometimes they are left for us to discover as a source of joy and laughter, sometimes they are simply a reminder that our heavenly guides or spirits are always with us and that often all we need to do is ask for a sign of their presence and we'll receive one. Many people are aware that white feathers are known to be a sign of heavenly contact, and personally I feel enchanted whenever I come across a pristine white feather in a completely unexpected situation. I always feel a warmth inside and keep these feathers as precious keepsakes of spirit contact. They are such a blessing to me.

> *Ever felt an angel's breath in the gentle breeze? A teardrop in the falling rain? Hear a whisper amongst the rustle of leaves? Or been kissed by a lone snowflake? Nature is an angel's favourite hiding place.*
>
> Carrie Latet

Heaven's calling cards are often there in nature around us – indeed it is the beauty of nature that so often reminds us of heaven while we are here on earth. Whether we might be gazing up at the peaks of the Himalayas or sitting by a babbling stream in the British countryside, nature is full of wonder.

Something that never fails to catch our attention and fill us with awe is the appearance of a rainbow on a shower-filled day, which is described wonderfully in Gwen's story below.

Somewhere over the rainbow

This story began last November. For my birthday, my daughter-in-law bought me a silver locket with angel wings on the outside of it and a tiny angel inside. My husband and I go to Portugal every year just before Christmas. We were sitting in a tavern we go to regularly, waiting to be served, while Maria, the owner, was outside serving other customers. I was wearing my angel locket and kept thinking that I would like to give the angel a name. When Maria came inside I asked her the name of her little girl. 'Bethany,' she replied, and I thought that would be perfect. It was fitting since it was so near to Christmas and reminded me of Bethlehem.

The next summer, one night in July, I asked God to let me know if he was near me and to give me a sign in the sky. I looked out of the window, not expecting to see anything, but was delighted to see an unusual rainbow. The top of the arc was covered in clouds but you could see either end.

I switched on the television and a young woman was singing 'Somewhere over the Rainbow'. Halfway through, she brought a young girl on and introduced her. 'This is Bethany,' she said, and together they finished the song.

Signs like a rainbow suddenly appearing are often given in answer to a prayer, especially when we are really in need of reassurance that things are going to be okay in our life even if we are going through major difficulties. Serena asked for a sign of encouragement while waiting for exam results.

A rainbow that foretold a silver lining

I am writing this email to tell you of my first wonderful experience of my angel.

A few weeks ago I was having lots of family arguments and was feeling very low and depressed. This was also a week before my A-level results were released, so I was feeling even more nervous and scared than usual. I was in the car crying when I said to myself, 'Angel, if you're there for me please show me that everything will be okay and will work out.' I thought of what made me happy and asked for a rainbow. The weather outside was miserable and rainy. In less than a minute, the sun came out from nowhere and shone brightly through the front windscreen. Due to the blinding brightness I was forced to turn my head to face the side window of the car. What I beheld was a little rainbow peeking out from a cave. It seemed to grow brighter and larger – so much so that everyone in the car began to comment. I was beside myself with happiness and said a silent thank you.

A week later (today) I got my A-level results. I got rejected from my first-choice university, Cardiff, and became very sad, but did not give up hope. Later this evening I got an offer from the same university for a different course but one that is even more tailored to what I wish to become in the future. It seems that it has all worked out for the best and I am very excited to see all the opportunities that will be available to me at university!

I was moved when I read your book *An Angel Spoke to Me* and believe that it found its way to me for a reason. The book, along with my experience, has given me a new-found sense of faith and happiness so thank you!

It is particularly encouraging to receive Serena's message that what she initially thought was bad news, when first rejected by the university of her choice, turned out to be even better news in the end with their offer of an alternative course. And given a lift by the appearance of the rainbow a few days before, Serena was able to be open to and embrace the silver lining of the situation. I think divine signs and messages from heaven are often sent to us to do just that: to show us that there are often wonderful experiences that come from unexpected turns in the road. The fact that we will never get to the exact spot at the end of the rainbow reminds us of all the wonder in this world; that our lives aren't set in stone or fixed into place but are fluid and full of fascinating twists and turns. Even out of terrible and painful grief when we lose a loved one, this is often the time when we grow as a spiritual person and begin to widen our horizons.

Like rainbows, the appearance of white feathers is a sign that so many people understand as a message of love from heaven. Just as I am always enchanted by them, Kim felt comforted by the unexpected and beautiful appearance of a white feather:

Calling card of reassurance

I was very worried about my daughter, who was having some financial problems. I was thinking about her while driving one morning, then as I looked down I saw a beautiful white feather on the passenger seat. I don't know how it got there, but it was as if I was being reassured, and in fact my daughter's problems were quickly resolved.

Joe also came across white feathers in significant places, and then had an extraordinary experience with the car radio:

Three white feathers and a misbehaving radio

After reading your latest book, *Celtic Angels*, and having read some of your other books, I wanted to share with you my own angel experiences.

Last year, I moved from London to Cheshire to be closer to my mum. She had moved from London ten years earlier and I decided that it was the right time for me to follow suit. I bought a new house and was just settling in when my mum suddenly and unexpectedly passed away. I couldn't believe it and felt numb and devastated at the same time. My primary reason for moving was no longer with me. Over the next few months I sank lower and lower into depression. I felt so isolated and didn't see the purpose or joy in anything. When I read in your previous books how you had felt at low points in your life I could really relate to your experiences and your words gave me strength to carry on.

It was not long after my mum's death that I started reading books about the afterlife and one day, while in the garden, I saw two white feathers. Not thinking they could possibly be angel calling cards, I picked them up and put them in the bin. I soon regretted this as I realized that I had not opened my mind to the possibility these had been given to me by my mum or the angels. My regret must have been heard because very shortly after that, another two feathers appeared in the garden – similar in shape and size to the previous ones!

Sometime later, on my mum's birthday, I went with some of my family to Mum's grave. And what was lying on the grass over her grave? A white feather. I have kept this and the two feathers that floated into my garden as gifts from my mum and the angels.

The next experience may sound quite bizarre and occurred not long after Mum's death. I was driving with my niece to the cemetery in my dad's car. He has a radio that you pull out when you are not in the car so that all that can be seen to any passers-by is the housing unit which the radio clips into. On this day, the radio was in the glove box as I certainly wasn't in the mood to listen to music. Not long after I started driving, my niece and I got the shock of our lives when music started coming out of the speakers. We both instinctively looked at where the radio should be, even though we both knew it was in the glove box. I asked in a stunned voice, 'Is this freaking you out?' to which she replied, 'Er, yeah!'

But this was not to be the only time it happened. A few days after that, I had just got into the car after visiting my mum's grave when the radio came on again and stayed on nearly the whole one-mile journey to my mum and dad's house. Needless to say, the radio was in the glove box. When I spoke to a few people about this, some said that it was possible for the housing unit to pick up a radio signal without the radio being plugged in, but I don't know if this is true. In any event, it had never happened before (and my dad has had that car a good few years) and it hasn't happened since. Coincidence? I don't think so. I'd like to think it was my mum's spirit and the angels trying to get through in some way when I desperately needed comfort.

Just to finish off, it was last night, after finishing your book, that I wondered whether I should write to you with my experiences. I got confirmation that I should indeed write to you when I turned on the television this morning. The programme information came up, as it always does after turning on the television or changing the channel, and the words that greeted me when I looked up at the screen were the title of a film – *White Feather.*

I think it's no coincidence that so many divine calling cards and signs appear in the sky. Jane was feeling a great sadness when heaven sent her a card of pure love:

A heart in the sky

I would like tell you about something that happened to me this summer. One day, while I was driving home, a deep sadness fell on me. I was going through a difficult time in my life and struggling to keep my spirits up. I'm sorry to say that I had an overwhelming feeling that I wanted to crash my car. Just at that moment I looked to the sky and I saw the dis-. tinct shape of a heart. On seeing the heart I immediately understood that I was surrounded by love. I was reminded of the truth that there are many people in my life who love me and who I care very much about, and that to live is the best thing that I have!

For Julia, it was through nature's wild animals that heaven sent her more than one sign.

An owl, a fox and a rabbit

I have just read your book *Angel Babies*, which I enjoyed a great deal. I thought I would share some of my experiences. Some of them happened years ago, but actually I have just remembered what happened when I had finished your book. I took it on a short trip to France the week before last, and what happens concerns the return journey.

A friend of mine, Jenny, died at the beginning of February – she was only forty-seven and had been living with cancer for ten years, determined to be there for her daughter, now nearly sixteen. Jenny always believed in angels, and as I drove back from France that night past her home town, I saw the hill near her home, with a star over it, and began to think about her intently. About ten minutes later, driving along the bypass, I imagined a large angel in front of me in the sky, and asked for a sign to be sent to me, that Jenny was okay. About two minutes later a large barn owl flew straight at my side window and had to veer upwards to avoid colliding with the car.

Still, I thought it could be a coincidence, so as I was driving along a country lane, I asked for another sign. A fox went across the road in front of me. I asked for another sign and a rabbit came out and dithered about in front of the car – I had to be careful not to hit it.

Some people might think so what, at 1.30 a.m. you are bound to see lots of wildlife, but to me, it was more than coincidence.

I noticed a similar thing when my partner's mother died. Considering we did not get on all that well, I had surprisingly vivid dreams following her death, including one in which she stood in a field, looking happy, trying to communicate with me. Then, when my partner was writing a eulogy for her, a Red Admiral butterfly behaved in an odd manner, persistently coming round us and settling on his shoulder for a long time. His mother collected butterfly brooches and her favourite colour was red.

Butterflies, and in particular Red Admiral butterflies, come up time after time in letters I receive about heavenly messages that appear at significant moments. I will write more about animals in the next chapter, which is all about enchanted moments here on earth, but I feel this is a good place to include a couple more descriptions of butterflies, as they are thought by so many to be a sign of spiritual presence.

Legend has it that when someone sobs,
Their tears are caught by butterflies and carried up to
*   heaven.*
Angels then float down as teardrops of comfort to take
*   away the sadness.*

Anonymous

A woman from York wrote to me and shared her observations of a Red Admiral during her uncle's funeral, which took place on a freezing day in winter, not when you would expect to see a butterfly dancing around the church.

A butterfly in the depths of winter

Some years ago my uncle passed away. He was very much a gentleman who loved the countryside and being outdoors at one with nature. He kept chickens, rabbits, cats and dogs and was always at his happiest pottering around the garden.

It was mid-winter when he passed away and it had already been a long, hard winter with lots of snow. I went to the funeral and was seated near to the coffin. Suddenly I saw the most beautiful Red Admiral butterfly flutter around and then settle on the middle of the coffin. I was fascinated by it, as you just don't see butterflies in mid-winter in a very large, cold church. It stayed for a couple of minutes, then circled the coffin twice before rising suddenly and disappearing. I believe it was my uncle, saying goodbye.

Helen's prayer for a sign from heaven also appeared as a butterfly.

Touched by a butterfly

Thank you for your words of comfort. A couple of days ago I asked the angels for a sign of their presence – I did not have to wait long. A beautiful Red Admiral butterfly flew into my sitting room through a half-open window. It flew up to me and then turned around and went back through the window. I was so surprised as I have never seen a butterfly in the house before. Later I put on one of my angel music CDs to help calm me down and noticed that one of the tracks is called Red Admiral!

For Rose, the beauty of a butterfly appeared at just the right moment, as she puts it so well, carrying a message of reassurance in a sad time.

Winged messenger of comfort

My mother died in January 2003. I was devastated, but went through the motions of making all the funeral arrangements and clearing the house. As I had trained as a florist I decided the last thing I could do for my mum was to make her floral tributes. I chose the best flowers I could and made a large white heart trimmed with pink ribbon.

At the chapel, the funeral directors took the coffin from the hearse and put the flowers on top. One of the bearers tripped and all the flowers fell off. I became upset because I thought they had broken them, and as they tried to put them back as best they could I was sure they wouldn't look as good. Suddenly, out of nowhere, a Red Admiral butterfly appeared. It darted about and rested on the flowers, then it came and rested on my arm. It was as if it carried a message of reassurance. Still to this day, Red Admiral butterflies seem

to appear at times when I am feeling down or having difficulties.

For Ildiko, the recollection of a morning filled with butterfly
encounters gives her a chance to connect with the memory of
her mother at any time.

Butterflies from Vietnam

I started to read your book *An Angel Changed My Life*, and
almost instantly the writing drew me in. I think I read 120
pages in one go. Although the stories are really beautiful
and I believe those wonders, miracles and life-changing experiences did happen, I still had doubts in connecting the
stories to the angels. I thought those miracles happened because the people who experienced them are very positive
and able to look beyond themselves and their own egos. I
have had many enchanting moments in my life but I didn't
think of them in any kind of divine way. I remember in my
childhood a dog who chose a toy depending on my mood,
a receptionist in Egypt who would be able to erase all daily
frustration just by saying, 'Every day is your day', getting to
know that the love of my life is expecting a child; these were
all life-changing in their own way for me.

It won't come as a surprise to you that I am writing to
say my view has changed. You wrote in the book about animals or birds that can remind someone of a deceased loved
one, and then I remembered something. My beloved mother passed away in the summer of 2012. We were very close

— she wasn't only my mother but also my best friend, my truest advisor, the person with whom I could laugh and laugh for hours.

Losing her was so painful that for the first time I decided to not spend Christmas together with family. Instead I decided to join a trip to Vietnam (I always wanted to see it). It was a two-week bicycle trip around South Vietnam, starting in Ho Chi Minh, visiting the Mekong delta and the Cát Tiên National Park, a large natural reserve. We went there first by bus, then we crossed by ferry to the headquarters of the park, then took another truck, then we walked through the forest with a ranger, who guided us to one of the stations located by the crocodile lake. The nature, the wonderful sunset, the ranger's wisdom, all made this day special. We spent the night at the station, and next day morning, as I woke up very early, I decided to walk around a little. As I was walking on a wooden bridge, I suddenly noticed a beautiful big brown and orange butterfly flying around me, then another one and another one. They were wonderful. Then as suddenly as they appeared, they flew away. I walked a little further, and the same thing happened but this time with black, white and brown dotted butterflies. As I was returning to my room, suddenly the most beautiful butterfly, a very vivid blue one, flew directly to me, following me, circling around me, flying kamikaze-style under the bridge then suddenly above my head, which made me pause and enjoy the show of the 'sports stunt' butterfly.

By that time the others had woken up, and while I was standing there mesmerized by the blue butterfly, the

Vietnamese tour guide walked by with a toothbrush in his hand, and noticing the butterfly, said, 'Whenever my mother sees a butterfly, she always thinks of my deceased grandmother.' I immediately thought of my mother and smiled. It was a beautiful day, and when I read your book, I suddenly recollected the butterfly, the tour guide, the day; and now I believe my angel does send me messages all the time, no matter where I am – messages full of hope, peace and love, messages that I am never alone.

It is not only through nature that we receive signs and messages from heaven. Sometimes it will be something as seemingly ordinary as asking for a car parking space when it's really busy and right at that moment one appears as if out of nowhere. We might ask for help with a problem at work and suddenly it just seems to be resolved. At other times we receive messages in word form, especially when we have been asking a question. A fellow writer friend of mine was experiencing a crisis of confidence and kept asking what her purpose was, only to hear a poem later that day being read on the television which had the line, 'All I have is words, which I offer to you.' She realized in that moment the power that words have to communicate, to help others, to inspire and entertain – that being a writer is a pretty great purpose. I couldn't agree more!

For Julie, it was a song on the radio that answered her prayer for a sign.

Tracks of my tears

I have just finished *An Angel Healed Me* and I wanted to share with you something that happened to me half-way though reading your book.

I always leave my radio on very low when I go to bed. After reading a particular chapter of the book I asked who-ever was listening to me to play a particular song as a sign so I could believe in the afterlife and that angels did exist. I dropped off to sleep and at 5.45 a.m. my partner's phone beeped from a message he had been sent, waking me up. The song playing on the radio when I woke was 'Tracks of My Tears', which was my brother's favourite song and I had asked to be played. My brother passed away when he was twenty-five, which was twenty-one years ago. I feel like my partner was sent that text message by the angels to wake me up at that moment to hear the song. It has certainly convinced me there is life after death.

You might see a message in a newspaper headline. Also, some numbers are thought to indicate the presence of heaven – the number 11 and its multiples (22, 33, 44 etc.) are often a sign that spirits are with you and are bringing your attention to their presence. For Stacey, she discovered a message in a car number plate.

A message from Blob

My name is Stacey. I'll start by saying your book, *Angel Babies*, has truly inspired me to connect with my angels and believe in them even more.

One particular angel experience I want to share with you is that of my baby who I sadly lost through miscarriage. I was nineteen when I became pregnant and was literally a few months into starting university as a paediatric nurse. At that time in my life, it was very difficult as I was dealing with several other issues too. I became very depressed and suicidal when I lost the baby, thinking it was my fault and I deserved to be punished. Still now it is painful and hard to accept. However, when I was about twenty-one, something very strange but comforting happened …

It was the anniversary of my miscarriage date, so I was feeling rather low that day with the usual negative thoughts and feelings. I remember driving back home crying my heart out thinking about my baby when suddenly a white van pulled out from a junction in front of me. I was about to shout in anger when I noticed something very odd. The van's registration ended in '8LO8'. As I didn't know the sex of my baby and I didn't want him or her to be called 'it', I had called the baby 'Blob'. The van's registration plate spelt Blob's name. After reading your book, I realized that this sign could have been my baby communicating to me, saying he is well and that I shouldn't feel guilty or depressed. I found this extremely comforting. The funny thing is that my mother has also seen this van. My mother was and still is the only person who was there for me while I was pregnant and going through the emotions of losing something so precious. I like to think that Blob was thanking my mother (his nanna) for taking care of me at the hospital and thereafter. My mother is still the only person I really open up to about Blob, which I love her even more for. It was an amazing experience I will never forget and think of on my down days. I find it comforting that my baby is still with me in spirit.

Valerie had a fascinating experience that involved not only words but also a form of technology.

Message on a Kindle

My husband of forty-eight years crossed over six weeks ago and after saying goodbye to him in the Chapel of Rest I came home tired and devastated. I decided to have an early night and as I climbed the stairs I said out loud, 'Please give me a sign, Fred, that you are still around me.' I went up to bed and realized that I needed to download a new book to my Kindle for something to read before I fell asleep. At random I chose your book *The Afterlife Is Real* and I started to read it straight away. A few pages into Chapter One I turned the page and a sub-heading was flashing rapidly and when it settled the words that were flashing read, 'It's Me'. To say I was shocked is an understatement and I kept turning back and forth and each time the two words flashed at me before eventually coming to a standstill.

When I had calmed down I thought to myself that maybe it was a fault on my Kindle or that maybe it had been designed to do this spooky thing, being as the book was about the afterlife. I carried on reading and about fifteen pages later the same thing happened. Two words of a sub-heading flashed rapidly, only to read 'Making Contact' when it settled.

I am so excited about this and would be grateful if you would confirm that this book was not designed to do this. I couldn't wait to write to you and tell you so I read your book pretty quickly during the following few days. The words still flash on and off but a lot slower now and I hope they don't stop altogether because it is very comforting. I have been showing friends, who are just as flabbergasted as I am.

A few days before my husband passed away I came home from visiting him in hospital and fell asleep straight away. I woke up in the middle of the night and in the semi-darkness I saw what appeared to be a white butterfly in the lower corner of the room. This was odd because I had been out all day and my windows had been closed. I turned on my bedside light and the butterfly came and settled on my arm. I then saw that it was actually bright yellow with a body to match. I kept gently shaking it off until eventually I shook it harder and it flew off my arm for good so I turned off my light and went back to sleep. The next day I looked for it and could see no sign of it anywhere.

The last thing that gives me great comfort happened in hospital about twelve hours before Fred actually died. He suddenly opened his eyes and looked straight ahead at the hospital screen surrounding him and smiled the most beautiful smile I had ever seen. He looked young again. He smiled this way three times and when I feel down in the dumps it is comforting to recall this.

Thanks, Theresa, for such a lovely book – I think I was meant to download it.

Sue also received an unusual message from the other side.

The afterlife is real

I have been reading your book *The Afterlife Is Real* and would like to share an experience with you:

I lost a daughter, Vicky, when she was three weeks off her fifteenth birthday, twenty-nine years ago. She was my precious first child. I have two other children – a daughter, forty-three, and a son, thirty-three.

About four years ago, on Mothering Sunday, I had just finished my dinner and had taken my plate into the kitchen to be washed. My daughter was still eating her meal. We did not have the TV or radio on so it was very peaceful. I returned to the dining-room table to remove the large place mats. I picked up the a first one and put it in my left hand, then reached to pick up the second mat and noticed there was a crumb on the table so placed the second mat on top of the first and reached for the crumb. When I put the second mat on top of the first the mats shook violently, I thought I had trapped a bumblebee or something between the mats, and at the same time I heard a noise like a text message dropping into my phone. I dropped the mats quickly on the table, expecting something to come from between them. I put my hand to my face and said, 'Oh that was strange' – my hands were shaking. My daughter looked up from her dinner and said, 'I heard it too', so I asked her what she heard and she said a sound like receiving a text. I checked my phone but there was no message. My daughter said it was Vicky saying Happy Mother's Day. I could not find any reason for the mat shaking or the sound.

The following day I told a colleague at work and she said that if my daughter wanted to get a message to me it would be in a way that I would understand and a text message with the vibration and sound might be the way.

I do believe in the afterlife but that was the first time I could attribute an incident to it.

For Minette, a physical book was just one of the signs that signalled the presence of heaven helping out her and her partner in their new venture.

Filled with gratitude

Ever since we started farming (as rookies) some eight years ago, I've been joking about how hard our guardian angels are working here keeping us safe. The more I said this, the more I realized that it was the absolute truth!

I became more and more aware of their presence all around the farm and especially on hilltops. It was as though they were watching us from a vantage point. Sometimes, when we had to work with a few difficult cattle, I felt their help, because things worked so smoothly.

One day I was shopping and was drawn to the paperback stand. I could not leave the shop without buying your *Celtic Angels* book. I was stunned to recognize many experiences as told by others. One evening I sat in my study; I remember I was feeling very upset about something, when suddenly a book fell over and yours was the one next to it. When I saw the title, I had to smile, because I knew my guardian angel wanted me to read it. After I read the first few chapters, it settled me down and I knew exactly how to handle the situation.

I am reading *An Angel Spoke to Me* at the moment and I am filled with so much gratitude – towards you (for sharing your experiences), towards all the angels in my life (for their guidance and love), towards my mom (who passed away in 2011, but who has helped me on countless occasions since she passed). Quoting from your book: it is critical for us to trust that this love and goodness will always be stronger than the forces of darkness.

Ann wrote to me with this lovely little story about how her mother-in-law seemed to show her presence as her son was in hospital writing a list after an operation, almost as though she was 'signing' her name.

That's my mum's writing

My husband Barry laughs about my beliefs but says he has an open mind. Anyway, I would like to tell you what happened when he was in hospital recently.

He had to go in for an overnight stay after an operation. His mother had passed away in February and as they hadn't been very close I'm afraid that few tears were shed. For some unknown reason I decided to wear a pair of her crystal earrings to the hospital the morning Barry was admitted. I didn't mention this to Barry or our daughter.

When Barry came home after the operation, he passed me a piece of paper and asked whose writing I thought it was. I immediately said, 'It's your mum's.' After his operation Barry had written a few things he wanted when he came home and he said at the time he didn't feel like he was writing it and when he looked at the list he thought, 'That's my mum's writing.' We asked our daughter and she said exactly the same thing and that she had sensed her gran in the hospital. We all think she was there looking after Barry.

For Esme, a message from heaven came through a special object that connected her and her elderly friend Pat.

The fire screen that found its way back to me

I have just read your book given as a gift to me by my friend Monica and felt inspired to tell you about Pat.

Pat was an attractive elderly Irish lady who was invited in by my mother for a cup of tea and was then officially regarded as our adopted grandmother for over twenty years. Pat had this special knack of making you feel better and her personality lit up any room. She would regularly pop in for tea two to three times a week and my mother would walk her home around the corner, followed by two of our cats. Pat would also visit Monica, our other Irish best friend and a Reiki healer, and have meals and chats with her.

Over the years Pat gave us many tears of laughter, especially as she often gave us out-of-date facial creams as gifts. One Christmas she gave Barry, Monica's husband who doted on her, a pot of Nivea cream with one half of it completely removed. After laughing so much my sides ached I then went home amazed to see another pot of Nivea on the dining-room table. My father told me it was his Christmas gift from Pat and I laughed my socks off when half of it was missing as well.

Both our families gave her many gifts over the years as she lived in a rented bedsit and we thought she could not afford much. After she died I was sad that her relatives did not acknowledge and thank my mother and Monica properly for all the care they had taken of Pat over the years.

In the last couple of years of her life I had helped her as best I could to alleviate the stress in her life. I gave her many gifts and one was a mirrored fire screen that had a picture of swans on it on a beautiful lake. I placed it under her window and when she sat in her chair opposite it became a room with a view.

Her death was devastating to me as I had bonded with her as if she were my own grandmother. It was a bit of an eye-opener after her death to discover she was in fact very rich and most of her relations seemed only interested in the inheritance. The vulture factor came into play and made me feel sick. The only item I wanted to remember her by was the fire screen I had once gifted her but I did not ask for it back as I found the whole affair vulgar.

Since she died I started to find coins on a regular basis and each time I found one I would place it in a miniature pottery Irish cauldron, along with a lovely card I once received from her.

At a local boot fair I stopped dumbstruck one day when I saw the fire screen I had given her for sale. I asked the price and was amazed it was only two pounds, far less than I had originally paid. I bought it back with tears in my eyes and a lump in my throat.

Also at the same boot fair at a different time I was staring at two Belleek pottery miniature cauldrons and asked the price. The lady said they were twenty-five pounds for the two. I thought silently to myself that if they were fifteen pounds for the two I would have them. The Irish lady leant forward and said, 'You were meant to have these and if you wish you can have both for fifteen pounds.' It gave me a warm feeling and made me smile and they now sit nicely in my kitchen, in my 'Irish' corner.

My family have some Irish blood in us and as I get older, I believe more and more in signs and angels. Just yesterday I opened the newspaper and it had a whole page on trips to

Ireland. This must be my future next step to discover more about angels, the Irish, and my heritage.

Thank you so much for your book *Celtic Angels* as it has opened my heart and my mind to new beginnings.

Esme didn't just find the fire screen that she had given Pat, but also came across coins, and this is another common sign of the presence of heaven.

As we have seen in previous chapters there are times when a sign from heaven isn't just to signify a presence or offer reassurance in some way. Occasionally spirits intervene in seemingly life or death situations, perhaps because it isn't our time yet. I know I felt both euphoria but also was very shocked when I realized that some form of divine intervention had in all likelihood saved me from a car crash when 'something' told me to turn in the opposite direction from where I was going. At the time I was just upset because I then missed an important appointment, but as I drove back later and saw the wreckage and then heard on the news that other people had lost their lives in the crash, I really couldn't understand what had happened, and why I should have been the lucky one. Now I just say thank you every day that my heavenly guides were with me that day.

As we've been exploring in this chapter, there are so many ways in which heaven can make contact and give us signs. As well as through natural objects like feathers, messages in words or numbers, sometimes heaven can be extra-resourceful when it comes to catching our attention. The following story is from Alice, who lives in Portugal.

The piggy bank that saved my daughter

I firmly believe in angels and, in my most difficult moments, I hold them close to me and they help in adversity so that things never look so bad. I am writing to tell you about an episode when, I have no doubt, angels saved my daughter's life.

I pray every night before falling asleep and always ask the angels to keep my girl safe. At the time this episode happened my daughter was five and I always asked that the angels would wake me if Luana ever needed me during the night.

Luana had a small piggy bank in her room that would play music when you put in a coin. One night between two or three in the morning, when I was fast asleep, I suddenly woke up hearing the piggy bank playing. I got up immediately and ran to my daughter's room to see what was going on, since no one had put a coin in the piggy bank. I grabbed the piggy bank and it just stopped playing. I checked on Luana and she was sound asleep. Everything in the room was in place. I went back to my room and I was about to get back into bed when I felt that something was wrong, as if the piggy bank suddenly playing like that was a sign that I shouldn't ignore. I went back to my daughter's room to check again. She was still fast asleep, but as I felt her forehead I realized she was burning with fever. My husband and I dressed as quickly as we could and rushed her to the hospital, where after several days and many tests they discovered that she had a serious kidney problem.

I have no doubt that the guardian angel of my daughter alerted me to what was happening – that an angel had called out to me.

Lily, a budding writer aged just thirteen, wrote this beautiful letter about her friend.

My friend is my angel

I was only four when I met my best friend, who strangely enough had the same name as me; we met at a caravan park and spent every second of the day with each other. This was convenient for my brother and sisters, for Lily had two older sisters – so did I – and one older brother – so did I – and we were all around the same age. Anyway, when Lily was born she had a problem with her kidney and had to have a transplant when she was two. She also had something wrong with her voice – I can't remember what she said it was, but when she spoke, she always spoke in a rough whisper. She had to take medicines every morning and spent a lot of time in hospital.

I was truly blessed to have a friend like her, but one day when I was eleven my mum took a day off work and decided to drive me to school so I didn't have to take the bus. I was really late for school and when Mum pulled over to let me out I asked her if she could walk me in, but before she could answer me her phone rang. It was my dad. When he spoke Mum immediately got out of the car and walked down the road a bit. But it was too late; Mum's phone was too loud and the words my father spoke still haunt me. 'Lily passed away this morning.' I sat in the car crying and when my mum returned we cried together. She let me have the day off school and I didn't leave my room for three days.

On Boxing Day that year an ethanol fireplace exploded in front of me and I was doused in flammable liquid. I was on fire and rushed to hospital. My mother said that I almost died. While I was in hospital they also discovered I had diabetes, but then the day I was meant to go home it completely disappeared, which was odd. Anyway, when I was lying in my hospital bed I was really scared and I was on my own because my dad had to work; it was 4 a.m. and I saw a blue light shine through the window. It frightened me but I felt somehow drawn towards it. Soon after, something fell off the table – it was the picture Lily's mum gave me on the day of her funeral, a picture of me and Lily. My mum came in just a few minutes later and told me that she had just heard a whisper in her ear calling her name and she said it sounded like Lily. She had felt suddenly worried about me and wanted to come and check on me. We both started to cry.

Now only ten months after that happened I still look back on it and think that Lily led my mum to me. I was grateful when Mum walked in because I was lonely and scared. Lily must have known and therefore must still be looking after me. When I first read your book *An Angel Spoke to Me* I had been crying about Lily just the night before and then my mum's boyfriend gave it to me and I instantly looked at the front cover and I swear the little girl on the front is the spitting image of Lily. I believe that Lily wants me to know that she's still here with me and she wants to help guide me through life.

It is lovely to see how, even at the young age of thirteen, Lily felt 'blessed' to have such a good friend; indeed our close friends really are our angels here on earth.

For Jan, the feeling that her stepfather is still present reminds her what a practical joker he was, almost as if he can't help himself now that he has passed over. Here is her story.

Sitting on a cloud laughing his socks off

I have to tell you about our 'poltergeist', who I think is my stepfather. He married my mum when I was ten. He was always a great prankster. After I got married he would come to visit me sometimes on his way home from work. If I was out he would let himself in and rearrange things. The ornaments, the pictures or the furniture. After the children came he was a great granddad to them and continued to play jokes. The children grew up and got married and still he was there playing jokes. He died in 1983 when he was in his late sixties, but still he continues to play jokes.

My daughter was reading in bed and her light kept switching itself off. After several times of switching it back on she said, 'Granddad, will you stop I'm trying to read,' and it stopped.

We are always losing things. To give but one example, I

bought a set of measuring cups and my grandson and I used them when making some cakes. We put them back in the 'cooking cupboard', but the next time I went to use them they were nowhere to be found. I turned the cupboard upside down but there was no sign of them. I checked with my grandson and he said we had definitely put them back where they were supposed to be in the cooking cupboard. He also turned the cupboard upside down ... still not there. We went out and bought a new set and when we came home and put them away there was the old set sitting on the shelf in the front of the cooking cupboard.

I often smell his tobacco smoke in the evenings when I'm watching television, so I know he's around. I can imagine him sitting on a cloud somewhere laughing his socks off!

Lauren also felt the presence of her granddad in the house and describes how she invited him to be at peace with them in their new house when they moved; that he didn't want to be left behind.

Inviting my granddad to the new house

My granddad died about nine years before I was born. I lived with my mum, dad and sister in the house my granddad lived in; I always sensed him around and would occasionally speak to him. I always felt safe there because I knew he was looking after us.

About six months ago we moved house and I felt upset

that I was leaving him behind. The people who moved into our old house told us that the back door kept opening by itself and that objects kept falling off surfaces. Even the curtains were opening and closing without anyone touching them and they kept hearing banging upstairs. I thought to myself, this is my granddad wondering where we have gone, so I went down to the house a few months back and as soon as I walked in I could feel him near. I spoke to him in my mind, telling him to come with me now to the new house.

Since then I feel him with me again and if I go down to the old house it feels empty. I'm happy he has found his way back to us again. Even though I never met him, I feel like I've known him for the last twenty years of my life.

Objects suddenly turning up out of the blue seems to be a favourite calling card. You almost feel like someone must be playing a joke on you or that you're losing your marbles – speaking of which, here is Annette's story.

Finding our marbles

I had a strange thing happen to me and wanted to write to tell you about it. It was 9 July 2008. I was in Egypt at this time as I knew my dad was dying – he had cancer and I couldn't bear to see him die as I was so close to him and loved him with all my heart. I remember it was ten past five in the morning Egyptian time and I had just got into bed when two bright lights appeared at the side of me and I thought, that's my dad, he has come to say goodbye. At that moment I looked straight at my phone, which began to ring, and I just knew it was my mum calling me to tell me dad had passed away. As soon as I answered I started rambling on to my mum because I didn't want to hear the words, but eventually I did and I hit the floor.

I still miss my dad so much, but something else strange happens now. We keep finding marbles in the bedroom upstairs and we know that no marbles have been brought into the house at all. They are always green, just like my dad's eyes were, and he always used to play marbles with me as a child.

I know the bright lights I saw that night in Egypt were my dad saying goodbye and I'm sure the marbles are a sign, too. It's nice to think of him still playing.

The following story from Mary is extremely touching: despite feeling very hurt about her relationship with her daughter she was able to find a real moment of hope on one of the hardest days of the year for her, Mother's Day.

A gift in time

Thirty-eight years ago I longed for a child. I particularly wanted a girl. Eventually, after a difficult pregnancy and birth, my daughter came along. My marriage was falling apart due to an abusive husband, but I got my precious daughter out of it.

Leann was the apple of my eye for years. I became a single parent. It was a struggle but I managed. Leann was a typical teenager, very secretive, and she grew further and further away from me. She seemed to resent me. Eventually when she was eighteen I met a wonderful man who was willing to be a decent stepfather. Leann resented him from the word go – he didn't get a chance.

However, she did like his son and a relationship began, although unfortunately this didn't last long and she cast him aside, which is how I felt too. By now she barely spoke to me; my new marriage was under strain but my husband loved me enough to ask his own son to move out and find somewhere else as he was the eldest and working.

Leann stayed living at home to go through college, but her coldness and indifference was by now making me ill. Eventually I told her she must go and live with her father. This was something she had threatened for years anyhow.

I hoped perhaps she would miss me, but she never did and never has. She got married and moved away, giving everyone strict orders that I should never be given her address. At my mother's funeral she sat on the opposite side of the church from me and everyone else and ignored us.

The years went by and I felt like a mother grieving although my child was still living. I dreaded Mother's Day. I'd see neighbours being brought bouquets of flowers, cards on the windowsills for all to see. Not even being in touch was the worst thing.

My husband would always take me into the countryside to try and help; being surrounded by beauty always made a difference. One Mother's Day, we were in a country park that overlooked a lake, but there still seemed no escape. Mothers and daughters were there walking along arm in arm, mothers and sons chatting away with each other. The hurt and feeling like an 'unwanted mum' just wouldn't go away.

We sat down on a bench and I felt I couldn't take it any longer. I couldn't understand why. I had never been unkind or cruel. It was way beyond me. She had never liked me long before it was obvious. I turned my head and out of the corner of my eye saw something on the arm of the bench. There lay a pair of brand new ladies' sheepskin gloves. I tried them on. My heart leapt, don't ask me why. I felt so happy. They were for me. I just knew no one had left them by mistake. I actually had something for Mother's Day too!

We finally traced Leann through the internet. She doesn't want me in her life or to see the grandchildren, which I am gradually accepting. It is a deep hurt, but an angel touched my heart that day, I am sure, and although the gloves may seem strange, I am a hundred per cent certain they weren't on that bench when I first sat down. Yes, I believe in angels …

Sometimes heaven will offer us a message in a calling card that reaches us through senses other than sight. Hearing divine voices or heavenly music is an experience that will often stay with a person for the rest of their life. To be touched by the other side in this way is an amazing gift, one that offered great comfort to Pat during a difficult time, so much so that it proved a turning point in her own healing process.

Divine singing

I would like to relate an unusual experience I had many years ago in my forties (I'm now seventy-eight). I was going through a difficult menopause, my father was dying of lung cancer, and then my severely brain-damaged younger daughter went into residential care. I desperately wanted her to go into a good home, as after twenty-two years of caring for her, which I was glad to do, I was mentally and physically drained. But when she went, I had nothing left to focus on and I didn't know how to go forward – I had always devoted all of my attention to her needs. I had never been able to relax even during the short periods of time when she slept.

So the end result was a bad breakdown for me. I felt fearful of unknown forces and kept praying for someone to help me. I even asked my deceased brother, who had died at eighteen when I was nineteen, to help me. We had been brought up almost like twins as there were only eleven months between us. Then I heard a voice in my head say, 'We won't let them [the dark forces] have you, as you belong to us.' At that moment I heard beautiful singing, but not of this earth.

After that experience, I began to gradually get well again. It was a long process, and every now and again I would feel mentally wobbly, but then I would remember the singing. As

I have got older I have had more unusual experiences. I hope this might be of interest. God bless you in your work, which comforts and helps people through the written word. It is a wonderful gift.

Christine also heard heavenly singing. Here is her story:

Heavenly music

Thank you for your book *An Angel Changed My Life*, given to me by a friend while I am at home receiving treatment for early stage breast cancer, which is going well. I am so privileged to have the support and encouragement of angels – long may you continue to enlighten and encourage with the help of these divine beings.

My tale though is not about now but dates back to July 2012. I was at home recovering from having a tumour removed from my mouth and we were waiting for news as to whether it was benign or malignant. Luckily it proved to be the former but took nearly three weeks after surgery before they could confirm this. Anyway, my hubby, Keith, was in the kitchen making a cuppa and I was lying down in bed when I heard heavenly singing. It was the most beautiful sound I had ever heard and lasted for no more than fifteen seconds, I suppose, but it was so clear and calm, neither in my head nor outside of it. I was totally mesmerized. When it stopped I knew deep down what it was and I mentally said I wish I could hear that again, and just as clearly for no more than a couple of seconds I heard the singing again.

The elation and humility I felt went very deep and I know that every day angels are with me, bringing me a calmness and deep-seated peace that will never leave me.

And for Grant, it was through the sense of smell that he felt the presence of his much-loved, departed grandmother.

Halls menthol sweets

My supernatural experiences have literally taken off since first my beloved nan, then my best friend and then my wonderful, unassuming father (who I can't ever recall getting mad at me once) passed to spirit.

My first experience was what I have now found out to be called an Olfactory ADC. My nan used to keep all sorts in her handbag and she always had a supply of Halls menthol boiled sweets, which believe me have a powerful fragrance all of their own. One day, maybe two to three years after my nan passed over, I was upstairs (on my own) in my house, which my nan had never seen because we had not been there long. I was putting away the washing when all of a sudden the Halls boiled sweets smell almost knocked me off my feet. This was my first ever experience (aged around thirty-four) that I could not explain. We don't even have anything remotely similar in smell in the house as these sweets never appealed to any of us.

A year later I had been in our upstairs bathroom and turned around and went to the top of my stairs and started a one-way conversation with my Jack Russell patiently waiting for me at the bottom. All of a sudden the towel on a hook next to the sink rose on its own as if an invisible person was drying their hands on it. After about five seconds it went back to the normal position. There were no windows open and no other people in the house. I had to go outside and pace the garden, thinking of what I needed to do but there was nothing. I was a little scared. It was then that I realized there are other dimensions on this planet of ours and something not visible to me had done this.

My father passed away in October 2011. I was given his mobile and that has turned itself on twice since his death. This considering that I have to dig my forefinger into it really hard to turn it on myself.

I love this next story from Marina; I think it is such a beautiful reminder that anyone may receive messages from heaven. She writes with perfect simplicity and really conveys what is at the heart of this book.

Things sort of happen to me

Over the years, I've had lots of strange things happen to me that I can never explain. I've known hard times, when money was very short, but I never told anyone. One day as I was walking to work (I didn't have the bus fare) I found a group of pound coins on the ground; another time I found a five-pound note. I felt my mum was looking down on me at the time.

Sometimes I may be sitting alone watching television

when I suddenly smell a really beautiful perfume or tobacco smoke. When I tell my friend I just say I had a visitor last night. She knows how things sort of happen to me and we smile.

Over the years I've had four major operations, with both knees and hips replaced. After the operations I've started to get very bad reactions to the anaesthetic and after the last hip replacement three years ago I had to have a blood transfusion as I had lost so much blood and they couldn't keep me awake.

It was while I was lying in bed that I opened my eyes and there at the foot of my bed was a lady in a beautiful blue dress. I can still see her, standing there, with her hands behind her back. In some ways it was like looking at myself. Was I having an out-of-body experience, or was it my Guardian Angel? I've never had a blue dress like that! You know in summer, when it is a really beautiful day with not a cloud in the sky and the sky is that deep blue colour? That was the colour of her dress.

I haven't any family now (I'm seventy-seven years old) but I do have some lovely friends, my collection of angels.

Marina also reminds us of the celestial helpers we have around us at all times in our lives, our 'collection of angels'. To be able to appreciate our friends as angels is one of the strongest messages that we can receive.

For Stacey, it was through reaching out and asking for help, which we should never be afraid to do, that she was given a message of divine connection:

Theresa Cheung

Just when we needed it

I went to a fortune teller and she asked me if I believed in angels; I said I'd never thought of it, so she said to me, when you go home tonight ask for a sign or a feather. I did that and a couple of days later I was standing in the front room with the outside door open and a feather just floated in and fell at my feet. I couldn't believe it.

About a week later I was in my bedroom all on my own and I asked for my angel's name; the name Tony came into my head straight away. I asked Tony if he could help in any way as I was struggling with money. We were down to our last five pounds. I went to the shop to get some milk and when I got home my partner set off for work in the car. Soon after, he called me to let me know he had been sitting in traffic and thought that for something to do he would look in the glove compartment, where he found eight pounds' worth of Tesco Club Card vouchers. I feel like Tony gave us a helping hand that day.

Friends are like angels who lift us to our feet when our wings have trouble remembering how to fly.

Anonymous

I would like to end this chapter with a beautiful poem written and sent to me by Pat King, who said in her letter that she feels inspired by the angels to write her poetry, showing that heaven can offer us beauty and creativity as well as comfort, support and so many other wonderful aspects of love.

Our Angel

Our Angel walks beside us
All through our life on Earth,
Our Angel stays beside us
From the moment of our birth.

Our Angel is a gift from God
Sent to us with love,
Our Angel watches over us
And sends our prayers above.

Our Angel gives hope and love to us
When we are sad and grieve,
Our Angel folds their wings around us
And will never, ever leave.

Our Angel guides and guards us
In everything we do,
We all have our Angel
Not only me, but you.

Pat King

CHAPTER FIVE

Lighting the darkness

Wisdom begins in wonder.
Socrates

This chapter will explore how the world of spirit can talk to us through moments of enchantment on earth: through babies and children, animals, other people and even our own words and deeds.

Let me start with a story sent to me by Sarah.

A life worth living

I wanted to tell you a little bit about how my angel experiences of recent times have really made my life worth living. Looking back, I don't think I would have survived without my angels although I thought they were just average occurrences at the time.

I am thirty-five, and last year I was diagnosed with breast cancer. I took this well, all things considered, but I also knew that six months off work would not be good for me. I am always busy and don't like too much time to sit around and dwell on things.

So as it happened, I met a strange man (well, I mean he was a stranger to me) at our local bar who then introduced me to his beautiful little bright white dog called Dil. He said it would be helpful if I could walk Dil for him as he was at work during the day. I had told him about my circumstances and he was very supportive. Dil became my little best friend. I have always dreamed of having my own dog and this was the perfect solution at the perfect time. We had beautiful walks in those six months, travelling miles and miles together, up hills and through fields, forests, beautiful gardens and by rivers and the sea. He is my angel.

However, it does not end there. I was going through a terribly destructive relationship but I realized that I needed to part from this person and live by myself. My angel supported and guided me through all of this. The very day I found the flat of my dreams I also found a white feather in my bedroom (I had no feather bed pillows or duvet, by the way). That was sign enough for me. Since then, numerous feathers have been sent to me through other people and come floating in front of my eyes. Beautiful little messages keep coming, however subtle, and I appreciate them so much. I feel honoured.

Three days ago I was walking Dil in the park and stood with him on the edge of the lake. There are plenty of lovely ducks around but the most beautiful, brighter-than-bright white duck swam around close to us and the sun shone down on him or her. It was wonderful because by this time I knew it was my angel but I would never have thought this before. At this point the duck swam right up in front of us with no fear like the other ducks, which all fear dogs. He floated there looking at us both for a minute or two then turned around, fluffed his feathers as if to say goodbye and off he went, leaving me feeling amazing.

My big question is, how have I been so lucky as to receive this gift of love? The last six months have been pleasurable instead of the harrowing depressive time that it could have been. I am now back at work in full good health and still get to see Dil and go and see the beauty of the world with him!

I have included a selection of animal stories later in this chapter but wanted to have this one at the beginning, not only as such a lovely example of an enchanted encounter when Sarah is introduced to the little dog Dil, who becomes a best friend, but also because of how Sarah sees this encounter as a gift of love, which I believe is what all experiences are that help us to connect with our heavenly guides or with the afterlife. Sarah was very brave through her illness, especially when she decided she needed to leave her abusive partner and live by herself. This isn't an easy decision to take even in the best of health and Sarah really used the strength and support that she felt her angels gave her during this time. And wouldn't so many of us love to have a little Dil in our lives, too.

Little pieces of heaven

As we have discovered throughout the stories gathered in this book, there are so many ways in which heaven may call out to us, whether we feel the healing or guiding hand of an angel, or we sense heaven at work in an amazing coincidence or flash of insight. We may be lucky enough to be given signs, in the form of feathers or clouds or even in the headline of a newspaper. And I think that children especially can be very sensitive to the presence of heaven; their hearts and minds are so naturally open that they don't close themselves off to noticing such things – they are curious and haven't yet built up the filters with which we adults tend to look at the world and our surroundings. Even those adults who I meet and who tell me about their experiences with the spirit world tend to have a youthful air about them and their attitude to life.

And sometimes I believe that heaven can call out to us through young children; children can offer us the gift of a message from above, or on occasion they become an earth angel themselves. The best way to explain this is to tell you my own story.

Quite a few years ago, when my son was just eight months old, there was a knock at the door. When I opened it, there was a young boy of just eight or nine years old, holding my son in his arms. I was completely taken aback; my son had just been playing in our living room. He could just crawl but wasn't yet able to walk and yet somehow he had managed to get outside and had been perilously close to some old steps that led off our porch.

The boy had bright blue eyes and a lovely smile, but I was so shocked and worried about my baby I must admit I snatched him back into my arms. A few moments later I remembered my manners and looked down to say thank you to the boy and tell him how grateful I was that he had there at the right time, but he had vanished. I rushed to the street to check in either direction, but again he was nowhere to be seen, even though the road was completely straight both ways so I really should have been able to spot him.

I know this boy could easily have been just a kind passer-by who spotted my baby escaping onto the porch, but whether he was human or in spirit, it doesn't matter to me because at that moment he was an angel.

Back in Chapter Two, we explored the relationship between intuition and the divine; how it is often with a little help from heaven that we are able to access our inner wisdom and to experience a moment of clarity in which we somehow just know what we are meant to do. I think that there is also a very close connection between the divine and our 'inner child'. Carl Jung even called our inner child the 'Divine Child', while Emmet Fox coined the term the 'Wonder Child'.

Psychotherapists describe the inner child as the part of you which is intuitive, and also playful, creative, spontaneous and passionate. And just like a child, it is also the part of us in the greatest need of comfort, reassurance, love and guidance. Our inner child needs to feel safe so that we can then fulfil our greatest potential with fearlessness and courage. I hope that by reading some of these magical stories about children and their connections with heaven you may get back in touch with your own inner child, because a young heart is one that is much more likely to be full of wonder.

If a child does have what appears to be a psychic experience, it can be daunting for us as adults, but to a child it will be the most normal thing in the world, and so the more relaxed we can be, the better. Children have an amazing degree of receptivity; when we talk about finding ways as adults to tune in better to the conversations we could be having with heaven, one of the best ways is to nurture our inner child, to let our imaginations run away with themselves more often. I believe as parents we should gently nourish and support this spiritual openness that children so often possess. It is easy to dismiss imaginary friends and children talking to thin air, and many adults might even be tempted to discourage such behaviour in toddlers. But if we can remain neutral then not only do we allow our children to simply be their natural selves, occasionally we may also catch a glimpse of heaven ourselves.

The next few stories are examples of just how open and receptive children often are to the presence of spirit. Natalie's son struck up a lovely relationship with his great-granddad even though he had never met him in this life.

He giggles when he is sleeping

My son Leon's great-granddad passed away a long time ago and Leon hasn't seen any pictures of him or been told about him yet as he is only two. While we were living with his dad and his dad's parents we would sometimes hear him laughing and 'talking' to someone in the bedroom from as young as four months old and from when he was born he would appear to follow something around the room with his gaze that we couldn't see. We could also sometimes smell cigarettes in the bedroom where Leon was (no one in the house smoked) so we asked Leon's nan if she knew what it could be and she said it could be her dad as he had always said he would make sure the people she cared about were safe before he passed.

Since then I have moved into my own flat with my son and the same things happen – he will follow something around the room and talk to it; also he giggles when he is sleeping, and even the cigarette smell is often present. White feathers have also appeared and I have found Leon playing with one a few times when he has been in his cot with all the windows shut in his room. We have also seen a robin on numerous occasions that appears to follow me when we go out. And during times when I have been very stressed coping with Leon by myself I have heard reassuring words. After speaking to Leon's nan I am sure it is her dad who is saying these things as the voice sounds just as she has described his to me.

Corrina wrote to share a fascinating account of her toddler daughter sensing not only that her granddad was in pain but that he needed a nurse.

Lucinda

My two-and-a-half-year-old daughter Lucinda was asleep one night and woke all of a sudden at 10:15 p.m. She looked out onto my landing, saying, 'Grandda', and I asked her, 'What about Grandda?' She continued to say Grandda a few more times then said, 'Granda needs nurse' and she described to me what a nurse's outfit looks like. I didn't understand it, and it wasn't until about 1.30 a.m. that she finally settled again.

The next day I went down to my dad's house and found out that he had felt pains in his chest just at the time Lucinda had woken up, and that they had stopped at the same time that she settled.

Children can be amazingly sensitive and receptive and it is as though Lucinda simply knew that her granddad was being helped out that night by the spirit world.

Brian sent me this deeply moving story about the beautiful ways his partner speaks to him.

Music to my heart

I just finished reading your book on the reality of the afterlife. I was very moved by it and it both confirmed the on-going experiences of more than a decade, since my much loved partner of nineteen years 'died', and provided one more extraordinary synchronous sign!

I am seventy-four years old, male, and have worked in the arts as a teacher and practitioner almost my whole life. I met my partner, Franck, during a residency in Pennsylvania in 1980-7, where I lived with him and then subsequently in Scotland when my artist's visa expired.

Although he died in Florida during my last visit to his winter home in 1999, he actually lived in Scotland with me, having retired from his post at Wilkes University (Wilkes-Barre, PA) in 1988, in order to be with me. So you can judge that our relationship was really very close.

I am not what would be called a professional psychic, however, I have a long history of such experiences which have supported me through difficulties all through my life. So, it was no surprise that after his passing, Franck lost no time in letting me know that he was still with me. We had in fact made a pact that whoever went 'home' first would contact the other.

Although he was ill with progressive heart failure, when his death came it was an appalling shock for which I was not ready at all! For the ten days of sorting out all the stuff that follows a death I went about my daily routine much like a zombie, and where Franck had been there seemed to be just an aching void. So by the time I got off the return flight at Heathrow, I no longer had any expectations. What sensitivity I had been used to had utterly vanished, or so it seemed.

As I trudged wearily to the baggage claim there was a blank in my mind and deep sadness. Then, like a sudden sunbeam finding a hole in a blind, I perceived a patch of brilliant light a short distance ahead of me and framed within it was a youthful and radiant image of Franck. I stopped in shock and in my mind exclaimed, 'Franck, is that really you?' The reply was characteristically irreverent, 'You bet your sweet ass!' and then instantly he was gone. From then on he has indicated his presence in numerous ingenious ways: often just a sense of his presence and a sensation like an affectionate stroking of the back of my head; but occasionally something more amazing: like the time while I was listening to Beethoven's Triple Concerto, its middle and lyrical slow movement, when I suddenly realised I was in an altogether extraordinary environment, as though a room had been hollowed out of a giant opal, with prismatic light glowing through it from all directions, and Franck sitting beside me rapt in the music! As I realised that this was out of the ordinary I was instantly back in my familiar surroundings and aware that the music had not missed a beat! And hearing a voice saying, 'This is an overlapping of dimensions'.

Reading your book, the chapter about signs, I was checking the list of possibilities to see if there were any I could claim, when I realised that the music I was hearing from the radio was very familiar, and for me charged with memory and emotion: the hymn-like tune in Sibelius' Finlandia. Franck loved this tune and would sing along with the words that had been added to create a patriotic song. In my mind I could hear his voice! So thank you for that! What an instant response!

I hope you like these anecdotes. As far as I am concerned there is no question that I can look forward to a reunion when my time comes. It is quite likely to be fairly soon as, like Franck I have some heart issues (aortal valve replacement last year). But as you can imagine, it is almost with impatience that I anticipate the event!

If you are interested, I have a website <www.briannobbs.com> where you can see examples of paintings, pottery, and some articles written by me.

God bless you for the work you are doing. It must be reaching and inspiring many people!

Love and Light,

You can see spirit

I was very interested to read your book *The Afterlife Is Real* and I thought you might be interested to hear of an experience I once had when I was about six or seven years old, living with my grandparents.

One morning I was getting dressed and had my bedroom door open. Suddenly I saw a lady coming up the stairs. She looked at me and smiled and then went into the opposite bedroom. When I came downstairs I asked my grandma who that lady was who just went up the stairs. She said she hadn't seen any lady and that I must have been dreaming. I was sure I hadn't been, so she sent my granddad upstairs to check. He came downstairs laughing, saying there really was no lady.

Over twenty years later I was living in Coventry and decided to visit a spiritualist church out of curiosity. The woman who took the service spoke to me and said, 'You can see spirit, can't you?' I replied that I didn't think so. She said, 'Oh yes, when you were a child you saw a spirit lady going up your stairs and she went into the opposite bedroom to yours.' I had no idea until that time that it might have been a spirit lady.

Michelle wrote to me a couple of years ago, to describe how she felt her father might have become a spiritual guide to her daughter after passing. She recently sent an update as she now has a little boy, too, who has so much of her father's spirit it's uncanny, and for Michelle, a great comfort.

The image of my dad

My dad was diagnosed with incurable cancer in October 2006. My heart sank when I found out, as I was only twenty-three and he was only fifty-six and the thought of losing my dad at such a young age made me feel sick to the stomach, as I was always a daddy's girl.

At the time, my cat had had two kittens. My dad disliked cats but I managed to convince him to keep the kittens as comfort for my mum in times to come. A couple of months later on, the kittens were chasing each other and one jumped up and smashed my dad's favorite ornament of an American Indian on a horse (my dad loved John Wayne and always watched Cowboy and Indian films). The ornament had been a present from me and my brother for his fiftieth birthday. At the time he was furious and threatened to send the cats away if it happened again, although I don't think he ever meant it.

A few months on, my dad's condition deteriorated and eventually, in October 2007, he became bedridden and was in a hospital bed downstairs in the front room. By this time he was unable to speak, just mumbling, and could barely see. Suddenly one night he started grumbling really loudly and shaking his head as if he was trying to tell me something. He began to point up towards the top of the cupboard near his bed, and there was the broken Indian ornament. It was as if he was saying, 'Get that fixed,' although I didn't read too much into it at the time.

Two days later my dad died. I was devastated. I had never felt so alone, even though I had supportive friends and family.

That night after my dad had died I stayed in my mum's room and in the morning when we woke up, in the middle of my mum's bedroom floor there was a picture of an American Indian, which belonged to my dad. We are both convinced it was a sign from my dad telling us to fix the ornament before his funeral, as there was no way the picture could have fallen down by itself as there was something heavy in front of it and it had been there for years. Anyhow, my mum and I set about fixing the ornament before his funeral.

After his funeral I had been asleep at my mum's in my room when suddenly out of nowhere my alarm clock went off and everything on my shelf fell off, all at the same time. It startled me as this all happened at midnight exactly and I never used my alarm clock. I felt calm, though, as if I felt a presence and it was my dad telling me he was okay and he was still there.

Two years after he died I gave birth to my first child, a daughter. Until then I always felt my dad's presence with me and as soon as she was born it was like he disappeared, as if he wasn't needed any more. However, there have been numerous occasions when I've been at my mum's house and my daughter waves towards my dad's old chair, which no one ever sat in except him, and smiles as if she can see someone she knows. When we call her name she doesn't even acknowledge us — it is almost as if she is in a trance and fixated on one spot. I remember that my dad always used to talk about how he would have loved grandchildren.

My daughter is two years old now and hasn't really done the waving thing for ages, but will still often go into a dream world and fixate on a spot and not hear us speaking to her or she will babble on to me about a man, who I assume she is saying she has seen or knows. But I obviously can't fully understand what she is saying as she's young still. Other strange things I've heard include times when she's been put in her bedroom for being naughty; one minute she will be throwing a massive tantrum with screaming and crying then the next she is laughing and chatting and saying hello as if she is talking to someone.

Could my dad be my little girl's angel?

....

I have had other experiences I would like to share.

Over the past year or so we had been trying to conceive for what felt like ages. It felt like it was never going to happen and it certainly wasn't happening quickly as it did with my daughter. Finally, in April 2012, I found out I was pregnant; we were both over the moon and following several checkups my due date was given as 24 December 2012. My partner and I didn't think too much into it but were glad as Christmas Eve is such a special day in our family, and was always my dad's favorite time of the year, a time of lots of fond memories.

Three months towards the end of my pregnancy I began to feel unwell, blacking out and having trouble breathing. I was admitted to hospital with a suspected blood clot in my lung and they had concerns that the baby might be suffering due to lack of oxygen. They tried making me have a scan, which would have posed a risk to the baby and increased its chances of having childhood cancer so I refused to have it. Usually I'm a worrier with things, but I had this overpowering urge inside, almost like an inner voice telling me as soon as they suggested it to say a firm no!

I was put on bed rest for the last twelve weeks of my pregnancy, which made me climb the walls, but on 24 December my baby boy came into the world safely. The birth was quick and he was taken away for oxygen as soon as he was born as he was struggling to breathe. After a minute or two they handed him to me and he looked the spitting image of my dad! It was surreal and weird but in a good way. I didn't say anything to my partner as I thought he would think I was going mad. It wasn't until the midwife asked us who he looked like that my partner said, 'He looks the spitting image of your dad.' It was nice to know it wasn't just me who had thought it.

Now I have a happy and healthy baby boy who is nearly ten months old. Recently I realized that my daughter was born on Monday 24 August, my son was born on Monday 24 December *and my dad was also born on a Monday, Monday 24 September 1951.*

At nearly ten months old my son is still the spitting image of my dad and sometimes I catch him staring at me with amazement, just how my dad used to, with a lot of love, and I get this warm feeling, as if it's my dad looking at me, if that makes any sense. I get great comfort from this as I still miss him so much, but looking at my son every day it feels just like my dad is living on and will always be close to me.

He's in the sky now

I was reading your book *The Afterlife Is Real* and got to the part about children being able to see things adults can't and I really wanted to share this with you.

I'm twenty-two and on 27 December 2012, I lost my husband, Adam. He was my soul mate, my best friend and the most perfect husband. I'm at the moment struggling still to believe what has actually happened as he was only twenty-nine and died of a brain aneurysm. We were so much in love and we couldn't believe how perfect it was that we were in each other's lives.

Adam had only one true best friend, from the age of sixteen. This was James, who married his childhood sweetheart, Caroline, and we all became friends. James and Caroline have a little girl, Leah, who is now five; they asked us both to be godparents and I was so honoured for them to also ask me as well.

When James and Caroline told Leah what had happened

to Adam, she told them that he's in the sky now. One morning, Leah was playing with her little brother and she said to her mum, 'I saw Adam last night,' and when Caroline asked her what she meant Leah explained that she saw him in her bedroom and he was standing with two men and that they went into Mum and Dad's room and so she followed them but then she couldn't see them anymore.

The strangest thing is that myself and Adam's family were sorting out the funeral arrangements and decided we were going to scatter his ashes at the same place as his granddad and uncle. So to me this means that he must have found them. That would be the only two men it could have been. This was not discussed around Leah or even her parents, so there is no explanation for her to think about or come up with the idea.

Your book is helping me get through this time and I hope and wish for Adam to come through to me and I believe he will when the time is right. Our love is so strong and I don't believe for a moment he will leave me on my own. We have been together four and a half years and we worked together and saw each other every single day of our relationship and I feel so lost without him. But your book is helping me to keep a lookout for signs and to believe and not to just find excuses for coincidences. So thank you.

What is so lovely is how matter of fact children will often be about seeing visions of those departed; heaven is something that makes perfect sense to them and that they don't need to constantly question or demand proof of; it's just *there*.

Natalie was similarly comforted when her nephew tragically passed away at just eight years old.

Where there is love, there is life

I have just finished reading your book *The Afterlife Is Real*, and I wanted to share my story with you.

Nine weeks ago, my eight-year-old nephew Taylor suddenly passed. We spent the weekend with him in hospital while he was on life support. Taylor had a brain stem tumour, which is, as we have now learned, a really aggressive type of cancer. We had to turn Taylor's life support off on Monday 18 February – just two weeks before his ninth birthday.

Taylor was such a loving child, especially when it came to his baby cousin Mia, my niece. The day my sister Sarah brought Mia home from hospital, Taylor cried; we asked him why he was crying and he replied, 'I'm just so happy that she's finally here.'

Since Taylor's passing, Mia (who has just turned two) has been talking to Taylor on a daily basis, and we believe she also sees him. She will sometimes walk into a room on her own and talk to Taylor; we know she is talking to him because she says his name repeatedly. She also tells us where he is in a room.

Two weeks ago, my sister Rachael (Taylor's mum) took Mia on a day out to see Peppa Pig. Mia was sitting in the back of Rachael's car in her car seat, and as they pulled away from us, Mia said to Rachael, 'Taylor's sitting in the front.' If I were to list to you the number of things that Mia says about Taylor and where he is, we would be here all day!

I find great comfort in knowing that Taylor is still around us and that he is okay, but I also found great comfort in reading your book. So from the bottom of my heart, thank you for teaching me that where there is love, there is life.

If there was one message that I would like for people to take from all of these incredible and very personal stories, always shared so generously and openly, it is Natalie's words that 'where there is love, there is life'. Amongst all the messages received from heaven, through angels and spirits, through wonderful coincidences or signs left on our path, even in the near-death experiences that we will read about in Chapter Seven, at the heart there is always an offering of love and a reminder that when all is said and done, it is love that is what truly matters. When we are able to embrace this reminder, it is as though life opens up before us and regains its colour and vividness.

Enchanted animals

We met Dil the little dog at the beginning of this chapter, who gave so much joy to Sarah during her treatment for cancer. There have been studies published which show that just owning a pet is good for a person's health and happiness. The act of stroking a pet, especially a cat or dog, reduces anxiety and can even have a beneficial effect on medical conditions like heart disease or high blood pressure. And owning – or in Sarah's case borrowing – a pet can prevent feelings of loneliness and depression.

Beyond household pets, there are many examples of how animals have come to the aid of humans, from dolphins who have saved swimmers from drowning to a cow that saved a little boy from being bitten by a snake – it blocked his path to prevent the boy from going near the snake. I remember a wonderful story of a toddler falling into a gorilla enclosure – gorillas can be extremely dangerous and aggressive but one of the female gorillas carefully picked up the toddler, cradled him in her arms and took him to the entrance of the enclosure so that the zoo keepers could retrieve him without him coming to any harm. Dolphins are known to be very spiritual mammals and a few years ago I had the opportunity to swim with Leister the dolphin – it was one of the most magical experiences of my life. Another friend of mine told me her own dolphin story – she was on holiday on a very quiet island in Florida and each day would wander out to the jetty at the end of the island. Occasionally she would spot a dolphin or even a few in a pod when she was lucky, but always quite far away. Then on her last day she decided to get up at dawn and walk out to the jetty to watch the sunrise. As she sat there it felt like she was the only person in the world, surrounded by nature. It was so quiet, just the gentle sound of a calm sea. And then out of nowhere a dolphin came right up to the jetty and jumped out of the water in a beautiful arc. It did a few turns and jumps and then swam off again. My friend rubbed her eyes – she wasn't sure if she had imagined what had just happened. But she knew it was real, and it's a moment of connection with nature that has remained a vivid memory for her ever since.

Psychic pets

I was lucky enough to get the chance to write a whole book devoted to psychic cats. As is so often the case in my work, just as the book was commissioned by the publishers, I began to start seeing the psychic powers of cats very clearly for myself. It was only a day after my husband and I had decided to get two kittens, after years of going back and forth and always deciding against it, that my agent rang to tell me that the book was going ahead. I've always been a head-over-heels cat lover and so I was thrilled.

We had decided to adopt two kittens or cats from either the RSPCA or Battersea Dogs and Cats Home; it took ages for us all to decide but eventually we chose two black kittens. Unfortunately we couldn't take them straight home as they were recovering from a stomach bug and so we went home and hoped they would get well soon.

The morning we were due to pick up the kittens I had the most vivid dream, in which two cats – one grey, the other ginger and cream – were licking my hand. Then, as we drove to the cattery that day, I had a bad feeling that I just couldn't shake off. It turned out that the two black kittens had been abused before being saved by the RSPCA and really needed very careful attention to rehabilitate, a different kind of care than we could truly offer having two young children. My husband

and I knew the children would be upset, but we also knew it was better to make the right decision sooner rather than later and so we broke the news that we would have to continue our search.

I couldn't believe it but the first picture I came across while searching the internet for cats that were in need of a home was of three Persian-cross kittens, two grey and one ginger and cream. We rang the breeder straight away and arranged to visit the kittens, by which time one of the greys had already been taken. The other one was a tiny thing, tumbling all over the place and such a heartbreaker – he came straight up to us, purring away. We were smitten and these two cats, Merlin and Max, had found their proud new owners.

It's been quite a journey with these two new members of our family – not all smooth sailing, with illnesses and behaviour issues we had to handle as best we could. But I'll never forget that dream of the two cats licking my hand. I can't help but think we were meant to all be a family.

John also felt like he was 'chosen' by his cat, rather than the other way around. And that little cat, Cola, turned out to be the perfect companion just when he needed a friend.

I was in love

I had never wanted a pet, but my girlfriend at the time was really keen and so I decided to buy her a puppy. It was a spur-of-the-moment thing, which I hadn't thought through and turned out to be a crazy idea. The puppy was beautiful and very cute, but chewed through everything in our flat and what he didn't chew he peed on. I felt terrible but we really weren't prepared for the responsibility of a puppy and so I took him back to the breeder, who I'm thankful to say found a lovely home for him very soon after.

A month later my girlfriend came home with a tiny tabby kitten. She was so shy, we could hardly coax her out from under the bed long enough to eat before she went straight back under. Soon after, my girlfriend and I split up; she left me and the little kitten behind in the flat even though technically she was hers. I remember that first night so well: I'd fallen asleep on the couch and woke up to see a little kitten looking up at me intently. I fed her and then, amazingly, she wandered back to the living room rather than going under the bed and she jumped up to sit on the couch next to me. I was in love.

From that moment on, Cola and I were inseparable around the house. She would follow me from room to room and curl up near me at night. That night she decided I belonged to her and I'm happy she did.

For some owners, their cat's psychic abilities go beyond being able to sense their emotions and I have received stories of cats seemingly being able to sense spirits. Gary wrote to me to tell me about his cat, Speck: apparently one evening the lights began to flicker in his living room and Speck jumped a mile high, and then just stared at a spot on the ceiling and meowed and hissed. Similarly, Donna wrote to share a tale about her cat Jessie who would 'talk' to the corner of the room when there was nothing there. She said that at other times Jessie would seem to watch something coming down the stairs, then run over to the bottom of the stairs and purr loudly. Donna liked to think of it as Jessie having 'friends in high places'.

Elaine also wrote to me with her fascinating story.

Snoring together

My dad used to go and visit my brother, Sam; he would always sit in the same chair while Sam worked on his research papers and occasionally he'd doze off, at which point Sam's cat Philip would jump up onto his lap and they would end up snoring away together.

We had always known that Mum and Dad wanted to be buried together. Mum had died a few years before, and when we lost Dad we knew we must fulfil their wishes. But what was so strange was that between Dad's death and the funeral, Philip the cat wouldn't go anywhere near the chair where Dad always sat while visiting my brother. If he got too close his hair would stand up on end. But as soon as we had the funeral, and Dad was indeed buried next to Mum, Philip jumped right up on Dad's favourite chair, snuggled up and dozed off.

Jeanne wrote to tell me about a few experiences she has had through her life, and I love her story about her dog Punch's spirit sitting by her husband in his usual spot.

Waiting for a foot massage

I have long believed that we survive physical death and have been fortunate enough to have a number of personal experiences that have strengthened my belief. I should like to tell you about some of them.

In your book, you mention the spirit return of pet animals. A few days after one of my dogs died, I 'saw' him standing close to my husband who was sitting in the armchair with one leg crossed over the other. I glimpsed the dog only briefly; just long enough to register that he had positioned himself over my husband's raised foot, just as he always used to do in order to have his chest massaged by that same foot!

This dog was called Punch, named after one that had once been owned by my grandmother. My grandmother and I were very close. Many years after her passing, I was walking Punch in our local park. I was in a relaxed frame of mind, not thinking of anything in particular, and certainly not of Grandma, when suddenly I saw, superimposed onto our doctor's house (it backed onto the park), an image of my grandmother's house. It wasn't until later that I was struck by the fact that the doctor's house number was 161 – the same as hers.

I think it was her way of communication with me, and it seems significant that of all my dogs, it was Punch who was with me at the time.

Sometimes visions appear in my head like waking dreams.

In one such, I was warned that my then toddler son was in danger. He was, I thought, asleep in his bed that particular evening when I suddenly 'saw' him, not in his room but in my bedroom. In the vision he was standing on a chair beneath the window with his hand on the latch. With this image came such a sense of urgency that I felt compelled to race upstairs, despite the doubts of my logical mind that what I was seeing could be real. I remember gasping at the scene as I switched on the bedroom light. It was exactly as I had seen in my head! There was my son, about to open the window. I had not heard a thing before this happened.

Incidentally, when I first met my husband of forty-seven years, I 'recognized' him, even though we had never met, and just knew that we would marry. It was love at first or, in this instance, second sight!

Sadly, Rachel had to leave her dog, Judy, when she left her husband, but Judy still managed to say goodbye in her own special way months later.

Judy

I was very unhappily married to a man who was a thug and a bully. In 1990, I finally gathered my courage and my children and left him. We had a dog named Judy. She was a Border Collie cross, and she had come to us as a puppy about ten years earlier.

Because I didn't have a home to go to when I left my husband, I sadly could not take her with us. Not long after the children and I had left, I heard that she had run away. Part of me was very sad to hear this, but another part of me was relieved because my husband had often hit her. I desperately hoped that she had found another home with someone who cared for her.

After a few months the children and I left the homeless persons unit and we were placed in temporary accommodation. Early one morning when I was fast asleep, I felt Judy stick her nose under my duvet and nudge me awake. She often used to do this when she wanted to be let out into the garden, or just to say, 'Wake up!' I turned over to pat her head and say hello to her. She was not there at all. I knew at once that she had left this world and had come to say goodbye. I had always hoped that one day she would understand why we had to leave her behind, and I believe that she came to let us know that she did, and that she was okay.

For Natasha, the love she felt for her dog and her puppies came through in her intuition and her prayers.

Miracle puppies

When I was eighteen years of age my dog Nickeeta had some beautiful puppies. They were so tiny and so very cute. I patted her on the back and told her what a good girl she had been and how she would make a wonderful mother to the puppies.

About two or three months after Nickeeta's pups were born I sat playing with them and giving them lots of love and care when I suddenly felt a tightening feeling in my stomach. I had a strong gut feeling that something was wrong with the puppies.

I asked my mother if we could take them to the vet for a check-up. She told me to stop being so silly as the pups looked perfectly well and happy. Still I could not shake the feeling that something was not right.

Two days later we woke to find all six puppies were extremely ill and looked as though they would not make it through the day. We took the pups straight to the vet and we were told that they had tick bite fever. The vet told my mother that the pups would have to be put down as there was nothing he could do to save them.

My heart felt as though it was made of brittle glass and had been thrown to the ground, causing it to shatter into a thousand pieces. I began to sob my heart out for our puppies. I thought of the pain Nickeeta would feel losing her babies. I thought of their little lives being cut so very short. It all felt wrong and I suddenly had this deep hunger in me to save them. 'It is not their time to go' were the words that kept ringing in my ears over and over again.

I suddenly found myself begging my mother to please take the puppies home and give them a little more time. I pleaded with her not to put them to sleep but to give it another day or two. The vet told me that he would be surprised if they made it till the next morning. But still I pleaded and cried so much that my mother eventually said okay and we took the puppies home again. I can remember thanking God all the way back for letting the puppies come home with us.

When we got home I sat for hours and hours with the six puppies. I cradled them in my arms, cried with them and prayed with all of my heart. That night I gave each puppy a loving hug and kiss then went to bed. I remember waking up hourly to check on them and make sure they were okay. The next morning we were totally amazed to wake up to happy barks. To our amazement the pups were running around happily playing chance and Nickeeta had a proud and grateful look on her face. We took them straight back to the vet to be checked over again. The vet was amazed and looked at us in disbelief. 'The puppies are a hundred per cent fine. I really do not understand it. I was convinced that they would not make it through the night.'

I could understand it. They got a second chance at life and they lived it well. All six pups grew up to be healthy and happy dogs. Nickeeta had her babies back and also went on to have many more happy little puppies.

Julie from Adelaide, Australia, wrote to share her story about Monty.

Monty and the monk

Most of my life I have had encounters with the afterlife. One that happened only recently was with a beloved pet of mine called Monty – a grey and white bits-of-everything dog. This is our story.

Monty had a history. I was actually her third owner. Her first owner was a young woman in her early thirties, Jane, who died of breast cancer. Jane gave her parents Monty to look after, Mr and Mrs Brown. Well, one day while walking down the street I saw a tall old man walking a grey dog with a noticeable limp. Mr Brown said hello and gave me a loving smile, which I reciprocated as I leant over and patted the dog. Mr Brown told me that unfortunately he and his wife were both unwell and so they were going to have to sell their house and that Monty had to be put down as the RSPCA said she was too old and unwell. I asked Mr Brown if he wouldn't mind telling me where he lived and that I would see if I could find an owner for Monty; he was pleased with my gesture and gave me their address.

I went off on my business again. Then I started thinking there was no way I would be able to have Monty come to live with us (which had been my first thought) as we already had four dogs. Surely it would be crazy to have another one; my thoughts were racing at this time and I felt eager to find Monty a new home fast.

Two days passed. I couldn't find anyone wanting an old dog, so I went to the Browns' home, knocked on the door and let them know that I was so sorry but that I had been unable to find an owner for Monty. Then I couldn't stop myself and said to them, 'Look, I tell you what, if Monty comes to me when I call her I'll take her home with me and have dog number five, but if she doesn't I won't take her as she looks very scared and is shaking, so maybe it's best she stays where she is.' I tried every trick in the book to convince her to come to me, but it was no good. I admitted to the Browns that she just didn't want to come with me, and I turned to walk to the front door. As soon as I did, Monty quickly dashed over to me and started licking my feet. The rest is history.

Monty got on brilliantly with her new friends, our other dogs – they loved her and she was soon boss of the house and knew exactly where she wanted to sleep: right next to my bedroom door with her large blue pillow and white baby blanket.

We had a great time together with the other dogs, going to parks, the beach and on lots of drives. I soon learned she had been beaten up quite badly when a burglar came to rob the Browns' home and that was what left her with a limp. All I can say is that Monty was different from the other dogs – she knew everything I was saying and was like another daughter to me. I was so very proud of my scruffy, limping dog.

I was blessed to have Monty for nearly five years until one day I saw her vomiting blood. I had no car so I picked her up, and walked for over an hour with her in my arms to the vet. It was a very hot day. I talked to her all the way, while Monty stared at me with these brown-blue eyes she had. I could see she was very ill, but I was determined to keep walking.

The vet said they would keep her in and do blood tests and so on. The next morning I received a call to come and pick Monty up as she was frantic and wanted to come home. I took her home, where she was eager to jump out of the car and see her doggy friends; she went up to all of them and it was as though she was whispering in their ears

– it seemed like this to us anyway. But then she started to vomit blood again so my daughter and I jumped into her car and took her straight back to the vet.

Sadly, the vet had to put Monty down later that evening. My daughter and I cried furiously as we comforted her beforehand with her favourite blanket – even then her tail started wagging.

For many weeks afterwards, it felt like my heart was broken. About a month later, still feeling bad and fighting tears, I had an urge to go to the city. I remembered there was a bookshop I used to like there and thought maybe this would be a good distraction for me. My daughter drove me to the city that morning and I went straight to the bookshop. It was peaceful, there was beautiful music playing and a large couch where you could sit and read. There was even a very large fountain inside, just as you walked in, and candles and statues; I didn't want to leave to go home.

I walked through this bookshop, enjoying the peaceful, heavenly-sounding music playing and still fighting back tears. I noticed a statue about a foot high of a smiling monk. He was holding a bucket into which water went from a well.

This monk made me laugh for the first time in weeks; I though straight away that whoever had made this monk had done so with much love. I thought he was beautiful, but that the price was too much for me to pay. I started to walk away, but I had to go back and buy the little monk after all. I also had the urge to walk home – I didn't want to catch the bus and I didn't want to ring my daughter to pick me up, I just needed to walk home, even though it was two and a half hours away. I passed a big cathedral and had my monk blessed there and stayed praying for a little while. I felt better so I carried on my journey home.

Now and again, as I made my way home, I would pull back the wrapping from the monk's face and smile again – his brown-blue eyes were so real he made me happy. When I reached home I unwrapped Monk and put him in the dining room where Monty loved to sit in the sun during the day.

When my daughter came home I showed her Monk and told her, 'Look at his eyes, they are an amazing brown-blue.' She looked, but said they were dark brown, almost black. I took him outside to check and realized they were indeed dark brown.

I thought I was going crazy, but then it struck me that it had almost been as though I had needed to relive the day I walked with Monty in my arms to the vet. The monk had had the same colour eyes as her all day, but here they were, completely different. This little statue had brought me so much closer to finding peace with what happened.

A few days later I went to my letter box to get some post and there on the ground I found two baby pure white feathers. I have never seen baby white feathers like this. I picked them up, smiled and took them inside. I placed them in the little monk's bucket.

Pets can make the most wonderful companions and sometimes they really are a best friend. So when we lose a pet it can feel as painful as losing a friend or family member. For Karen, although it was very upsetting to lose her dog, she was hugely comforted by her continuing presence.

A special friend

Since I lost my greyhound I have experienced something that never happened to me before. Sadly, my dog deteriorated quickly with illness when she was twelve years old. When she lost the use of her back legs after just a matter of weeks, I knew she was in a great deal of pain and I made the difficult decision to have her put to rest.

Since the day she died, I felt a presence in and around the house. I have been in the garden, looked up and seen the shape of her head in a cloud – even the right colouring and shading. When I have been thinking of her, and talking to her, a feather has dropped right down by my feet. When I went to the sea the other week exactly the same thing happened again. Occasionally, on a dull day, I have been wishing for her to be there and a bright light has shone through the clouds. This has also happened at night, a light coming through the curtains.

I thought it was just wishful thinking but I do feel it is as though she is telling me I haven't lost her altogether – that she is still keeping an eye on me. In her last days, I remember there was a great deal of eye contact. I believe these signs are a very special gift, whatever their meaning, a reminder of the bond and friendship that we had and still do.

As well as pets like cats and dogs, with which it makes sense that we might continue to have a strong connection even when they have passed, I often receive stories that feature birds and how they appear as celestial messengers, often with the spirit of a departed loved one.

For Lynne, the appearance of a young and vulnerable robin at her side brings to mind her father's love for her, even though they had a troubled relationship.

I remember the good times

My father's favourite bird was a robin, and robins have featured in my life in amazing ways. One late summer I was walking down a quiet road when I heard a trilling, chirruping noise that seemed to be following me as I walked along. I turned round to see a young robin, too young to be away from its parents. I ushered the little bird into a garden and hoped its mother would come and find it before long.

My father came from a broken home, abandoned at just three years old and brought up by his aunt in a tiny Welsh village. I will never know why he was so violent to me and I never asked. It's complicated, but when I saw that robin I felt his own vulnerability and I remember the good parts, the fun times and his love for me.

Teresa found a similar feeling of reassurance in the sudden appearance of a pair of blue tits.

Two little birds, side by side

A few years ago we moved to Italy. I had been through a particularly difficult and stressful time including the recent death of my mother's brother, the last of my relatives, whom I had looked after for over a year. I kept wondering what my parents would have thought about our new home in Italy.

One day, about a month after we arrived, I was standing by the open window in our bedroom, putting on my make-up at the dressing table, when suddenly there was a great fluttering of wings and there, side by side, were two little birds – blue tits. They hovered there, the pair of them, for several minutes, looking directly into the room from the middle of the open window. Even though they could see me there at the dressing table, they weren't frightened and didn't fly away. I am convinced it was a message from the other side – my deceased parents saying everything would be okay.

Dinah's heavenly animals are not what you might expect. They include a rhinoceros, a horse, a tiger and an eagle, amongst others. This is a vividly recounted story that shows just how strong the connection is between animals and humans, when we allow and encourage it to be a partnership rather than a case of man dominating other species.

A rhino behind me

When I was seven years old, I was taken on a school trip to London Zoo. One of the 'highlights' of the trip was to see Guy the Gorilla. I looked into his eyes and just saw incredible pain and anguish – it was so sad. Since that moment I always loathed zoos and never visited one again until my partner persuaded me that we should really take our children. The couple of times we did I felt all the animals' pain.

Life was becoming harder and harder and I remember at one time I was getting a lot of nasty comments from some people. I was feeling very down when I suddenly sensed, in spirit, a rhinoceros around me. The message I took from him was that I needed to grow a 'thick skin' when it came to these comments; that he would protect me and give me strength. When I attended the spiritualist church that week, the medium looked at me and laughed. He said he could see a rhino behind me.

Over the years, many other wild animals have shown up to help me out: a horse, tiger, black panther, bear, lion, wolf and an eagle. I call them my Angel Animals. Once I was reading a book by a medium who described a spirit who said he was with a group of boy spirits who needed our prayers and love as they had been ill-treated and unwanted during their lives. I thought of all the animals that had been neglected too and thought how wonderful it would be if the animals could go to the boys and they could help each other as companions looking out for one another. As soon as I thought it, I felt it happen, all the animals rushing to the boys. What joy.

Spirit sightings

Later in this chapter I want to share some stories about how spirits sometimes appear to us through humans – for example when a mysterious stranger suddenly appears, perhaps to give us a message or to offer us protection or help in our moment of need. Then there are those who believe they have seen spirits and angels on earth. In most cases this is when a person is visited by a departed loved one, or experiences a vision of them, as was the case with Rosemarie.

A sign my brother was happy

It was 1995, two weeks before my wedding, when my only brother, Oliver, died in an epileptic seizure. I was devastated as he was my only sibling, but even though I was in shock, going ahead with the wedding felt like the right thing to do, as Oliver would have wanted it.

Five years later I was on a pilgrimage to Lourdes as a member of a choir. We had a busy schedule but we managed to have one afternoon off and I decided to take part in the candlelit procession. During this time a vision of my brother Oliver appeared, first to the side of my line of vision, then across the front and over to the other side. It was a vision of Oliver smiling. I wasn't even thinking of him at the time. I shared my experience with one of the priests and he reassured me and said it was a sign Oliver was happy. It gave me a feeling of warmth inside.

After reading your book *Celtic Angels* I decided to put pen to paper and share my story with you.

Ian wrote to share his experience of seeing a glimpse of heaven; he was awake at the time but says it was like the most vivid dream.

The colours

One day I was working too much, and for a moment I closed my eyes just to relax. As I did, I began to see the colours orange, red and yellow and then they began to all become one, mixed together. I saw something moving within the colour, and then the colours all transformed into a person's face.

The next thing I knew I was looking down upon a hilltop, where I could see a man standing. Everything was still in orange, red and yellow, not the usual colours with which we see. The man held his hand up in the air and the colours changed back to everyday. I was able to move so that I could see the man from behind; he had two large wings moving slowly back and forward.

From that day, I have felt the presence of my angels; it is a great feeling and I try to work with them as best I can.

The following story was reported in the national press, but is such a lovely one that I wanted to include it here:

Ultrasound angel

In December 2011, Dee Lazarou went for her twelve-week scan. As the nurse put the ultrasound monitor to her stomach she was able to see that her baby was doing well, but it wasn't until later, when Dee was showing her three-year-old the picture, that she spotted the perfect image of an angel alongside the tiny foetus. It felt like a great comfort, and she sensed that her baby was being looked over and looked after in her womb. Months later when Dee went into labour at home she didn't feel afraid, even when her baby came before there was a chance to get to the hospital. The midwife wasn't able to get there in time and so baby Leo was born in the bathroom with the brave help of her husband and mother.

'His cord was wrapped around his neck and it was my mother who pulled the cord free. It was a nerve-wracking experience, but I'm sure that a guardian angel was looking over him to make sure he was delivered safely,' Dee reported.

Dee has kept the picture of the ultrasound angel very safe so she will one day be able to tell Leo about his remarkable entrance into this life.

For Linda, it was sensing the presence of heaven that literally and emotionally gave her a lift.

In my hour of need

Ten years ago I had an experience that remains vivid and memorable in my mind to this day. I was going through a very traumatic divorce. My ex-husband and I were in a custody battle for our two children, I was losing my house and couldn't have been at a lower point in my life.

I remember going into town one day and parking in the multi-storey car park; I was feeling very low. As I walked towards the exit, I felt I was being 'lifted up'. It was as though invisible hands had hold of me, either side, and as I walked I couldn't feel my feet on the ground, as if I was walking on air.

It was very surreal but I'm sure my angels were comforting and supporting me in my hour of need. I will never forget it.

Jennifer wrote to me with her story about how her dad let his presence be known by moving the furniture around!

He liked everything just right

I've read a few of your books and really enjoyed them, and I thought I would let you know about my experience after my dad passed over. I was always very close to him and he died when I was thirty-seven. He had seemed fine but was getting older and suddenly died of a heart attack. I was absolutely devastated as I loved him so much and knew how much I was going to miss him.

In the days leading up to the funeral my brother and I decided to decorate the living room to freshen it up as all the family were to meet there before we went to the church. We moved the furniture around and set to it – not really a very good idea as we were both very upset, but still we got the decorating completed. The night before the funeral my brother and myself stayed over at my dad's. I was woken at 5.30 in the morning by noise from the room below me, which was the living room, and I could hear the furniture being moved around. I knew it was my dad in the room below as he liked everything just right. It went on for about an hour. I never got out of bed, I just lay there listening to it. I think it was my dad's way of letting me know he was okay. I told my brother about it in the morning but he never heard a thing.

Occasionally people will see angels in full form, with wings and all. We might not always be able to tell if they are physically here or have appeared through a vision, but to be visited in this way always leaves an impression of wonder on the person. This is what happened to one reader.

An angel at the foot of the bed

About three years ago a very strange thing happened to me and I feel I should tell someone about it. I was lying in bed on my back in a darkened room with my eyes open when a glow started at the foot of the bed and it got brighter and brighter and an angel appeared. She was about seven foot tall, blonde and the clarity with which I saw her was absolutely amazing.

Nothing on earth could reproduce anything with so much detail and colour. She had a terrific wing span that reached to the corners of the room. Every feather stood out, as did the folds of her dress.

I said, 'Hello, what's your name?' She just looked at me and vanished. I hadn't had any deaths in the family for some time and I wasn't thinking of anyone in particular. I do wish it would happen again as it was so wonderful.

Visions will often be of someone about to depart or already departed, a message of love that usually says, 'Don't worry about me, I'm fine.' Death is still the great unknown and it can fill us with uncertainty and fear, or we can miss our loved ones so much that we don't know how to go on without them. Receiving a message that things don't just suddenly end, that our loved ones are happy and safe in their new home, and that we will never be alone, is one of the most comforting ways that heaven can communicate with us.

I love this story, sent to me by Dawn. Sometimes I think the smallest gestures of love can be the most powerful.

I'm going now, love

My mother and I always had that kind of unspoken thing in our relationship, where I might be thinking of her or want to tell her about something, and the phone would ring and it would be her. The same is true between my daughter and me – I might ring her and she says she was just thinking of me in that moment.

In 2000, my partner and I were running a busy village pub in Norfolk. It was during the summer, and Mum had been suffering with angina and was booked in for bypass surgery. I visited her a few days before her operation, but couldn't be there on the day because of the pub.

It was a busy Friday evening and I was flat out, cooking in the kitchen. The waitress was dashing in and out with orders, but I barely had time to look up from my work. I was frying fish in the fryer when Mum breezed into the kitchen and said, 'I'm going now, love,' as if she'd been for a visit. I was so engrossed I just replied, 'Okay then, love you.' It was just after eight.

About ten o'clock when service calmed down in the kitchen I tried to phone my brother in Sheffield for news of Mum but his phone kept going to voicemail. Eventually, my brother rang me to say Mum had passed away on the operating table at around eight o'clock that evening.

I knew Mum's spirit had come to say goodbye, and about a week later I saw her smile at me in the mirror. I never saw her again but sometimes I feel her presence around me, usually when I'm doing something I shouldn't be!

A couple of years ago, Grace wrote to me to share her experiences after her daughter tragically died in a car accident. What spoke to me so clearly in her letter was that her moments of connection with the afterlife had given her understanding without covering up the pain and loss she felt. I think this is one of the greatest gifts that the world of spirit has to offer us.

My darling daughter Claire

On 1 June 2005, my beautiful daughter, Claire, was killed in a car accident. She was twenty-three.

I can't even begin to tell you how much I love and miss her, so I won't even try. But I do want to tell you a few things that help me to remember that she is safe and happy, and that one day I will see her again.

When Claire died, I was consumed with a need to know where she had gone, and that she was alright. I started looking for a medium, and after a few weeks of going to various demonstrations at the Spiritualist Association of Great Britain, I found 'my' medium.

There are so many things that he has told me that could only have come from my daughter, which have made me cry and be comforted at the same time. One of these concerns the night she died:

I had been working late, and afterwards was having supper with my boss and his wife at a nearby restaurant. Just as we were nearing the end of our meal, I got a call from my eldest daughter. She was completely distraught and incoherent. She was on her way to visit Claire, who had moved to Wales a few months earlier. They were to meet in a car park not far from where Claire lived with her boyfriend, as my eldest daughter wasn't sure of how to find her sister's cottage. They had spoken on the phone and were due to meet up in seven minutes. They were both very excited to be seeing each other. My eldest daughter waited at the car park, but there was no sign of Claire. So she decided to try and make her way to the cottage as best as she could. On the way, she was overtaken by two fire engines on the otherwise deserted road. It was at that point that she called me to say that she was very frightened, and thought that something bad had happened to her sister.

I left the restaurant immediately and came home by Tube. As soon as I had a signal again, I kept trying to reach my daughters, but there was no reply. I got indoors and, still not able to reach either daughter, I phoned a friend to tell him that I thought something terrible had happened to Claire. As I was speaking to him there was a knock at my door. I knew it would be the police. I ended the call to my friend, but for some reason I kept hold of the phone and was holding it against my chest. I was still holding it there while the police informed me that yes, my daughter had suffered a fatal car crash.

During a session with 'my' medium, he asked me if I had been with Claire when she died. I said, 'No, I wasn't.' He then said, 'Well, I've got your daughter here telling me that she was with you, and comforting you, and you were holding a phone here,' and he pointed to his chest. He repeated again that Claire was with me, helping me through those first terrible, unbelievable moments.

Since that night, over eight years ago now, I have had some very dark times trying to come to terms with my daughter's death. But I have also found that although I will miss my beautiful girl until the time comes when I no longer need to be in this life, I do have a deep belief that I will see her again. I have also found that I have no fear of my own death.

Grace then wrote to me again to share this wonderful vision, in which she felt as if her daughter Claire was showing her around her new home.

A glimpse of heaven

There is one final thing that I would like to tell you about:

I have never been able to meditate. I have tried on many occasions and usually end up falling asleep, or my mind wanders off to the realms of shopping lists or hair-washing.

One sleepless night, nearly three years after Claire died, I decided to try some breathing exercises and visualized going up my mountain to reach the rainbow bridge, which is usually where I fall asleep. But this time, I had the most magical meeting with my daughter. It was so clear and beautiful.

I met Claire on the rainbow bridge. She took my hand and then showed me 'her' place.

There was a pool with many gentle waterfalls flowing into it. She told me, without speaking, that this is where all the love that we have for her goes. She bathes in it. Then she showed me a jewelled chest, and this is where all our memories and reminiscences of her are held. She told me of another place, which I didn't see, where our poems and writings about her are, and also our thoughts and questions.

Claire then took me to what looked like a summerhouse. Hanging on the eaves was a sort of wind chime made of beautiful colours and sounds. She explained that when we laugh, this causes the wind chime to move in a pattern of sound and colour that is unique to the person who is laughing. There was a fountain of crystal cups, each one containing the colours of our sorrow. The sorrow colours in each cup rise and fall and sometimes spill over, depending on what is being felt by us here who know and miss her. Some of the cups will disappear when they are empty, but there will be others that will always have a sorrow colour in them, and will only disappear when that person has finished their life on earth.

Inside the summerhouse was a divan. On the divan there were cushions of different colours and feelings. These pillows belong to those who know and love her. When we are dreaming, she can lay her head on these pillows and know our dreams. Sometimes she steps into these dreams; she 'told' me that she is still learning how to do this!

Claire also let me know that there are other places she goes to, to do different things with others, but that this was her own special place.

Then, I had to go back.

When I came back from this journey, I truly felt as though I had spent time with my daughter in her beautiful place. I wrote it all down as best I could at the time, but really, there are no words that can convey the beauty, and the feeling of love and complete acceptance that all was as it should be.

Thank you for your lovely books, Theresa, and thank you for the invitation to send you my experiences.

Theresa Cheung

On rare occasions, the visions that people see allow them to somehow cross the usual barriers of time or space. This is more common during OBEs (out-of-body experiences), such as in Chapter Three, or during near-death experiences, some of which I have included in Chapter Seven, but they can also happen while we are conscious and awake. Here's what happened to Patricia when she was a teenager who didn't think much of her world.

I knew my dad was going to save Adam

Back in 1965 I was a depressed, lonely teenager. I was bullied at school and didn't even like to pray anymore because I felt that God had failed me.

Early one evening I was standing at one end of our living room staring into space. Very vividly in my mind's eye I saw my dad walking from the hallway that led to the bedrooms into the living room. He was stark naked! Beneath one arm he was carrying my seven-year-old brother Adam, who hung limply at his side. My frantic-looking mother walked alongside them both. Sounds were indistinct if I heard anything at all, but I strongly sensed she was pleading with my dad to save Adam's life. A few seconds later they all vanished into thin air! I was badly shaken, and embarrassed to see my dad without clothes. It was two weeks later I found out why.

My father was in the bath when there was suddenly a crisis going on in my brother's bedroom. My mother had been tucking Adam into bed when all of a sudden he keeled over in her arms, totally unconscious. She screamed for my dad, who didn't have time to put on any clothes. When Dad emerged from the hallway with my mother and Adam, I was standing in the exact same spot where I'd had the vision two weeks before. I went with them into the kitchen, where Dad laid Adam on the table. He gave him CPR and mouth-to-mouth, skills he'd learned long ago in the army.

My older brother ran next door to ask the neighbours to call an ambulance since we didn't have phone service at the time. While my parents were at the hospital with Adam, I did something I'd never done in all my life: I went into my room and sank to my knees, pleading with God to save Adam's life. I didn't get up until I felt some sort of inner peace.

There was a brand-new doctor on the hospital team who worked valiantly to save Adam's life. For a while it was touch and go and later, my mum told us Adam said he saw 'birdies' in the air. Now I realize celestial helpers were getting ready to take Adam home but my prayers helped turn the tide, or perhaps it wasn't his time.

Adam and I got to be very close later in life and we'd spend a lot of time talking whenever I crossed the country to visit my family. We helped each other, and I believe we have always shared this bond.

In the following story, Natasha shares her experiences of how she had begun to notice the presence of someone she didn't recognize, who she has since considered to be her spirit guide.

Spirit guide James

In June 2009 I was going through a very tough time in my life and I felt so depressed and did not know which way to turn. I felt lost and afraid, alone and desperate for help. I then started to notice that there was a spirit following me around. Each time I felt really down and alone I would feel its presence comforting me. I would hear strange noises and whispering in my ear. I would also feel as though someone was giving me a hug, touching my shoulder or standing next to me.

At night I would feel as though someone was sitting on the end of my bed or a hand was resting on my leg. I was not afraid, as I felt that this was a good presence and it only appeared when I was feeling low. Each time I felt it I was left with a comforting feeling that I was not alone.

One day I invited a few girlfriends round for lunch as I thought it might help to make me feel a little better, having the company. A friend of mine called Kim came. She picked up on the presence instantly. She asked me if I realized that I had a spirit around me and I said yes. She said she would try to see what she could pick up on this spirit.

She said she could see a tall man who was in his seventies. He was in the army and he was connected to me somehow. She said the month of June was an important time for him. She also said that when he was alive he was a stern person who liked things to be kept in order. He was also a loveable and empathic person who used to make people laugh. I could not place who he was.

Kim then said that at the end of his life he had trouble breathing and she felt that he had died from breathing problems, possibly cancer in the chest and throat. The initial 'E' kept coming to her. She said that when I am down, this man will gently massage my shoulders to comfort me. She said there were many spirits around me, one of whom is an elderly woman, small, who had trouble standing without support.

I thanked Kim for the things she had said and then thought I would give it a go and see what I could pick up. I stood up and shut my eyes, asking for the spirits to talk to me. Straight away the name James came to me. I felt he enjoyed fishing and that he was lost.

A few days later I sat working at my computer when I got the strongest feeling that I was not alone. I could feel a presence standing next to me. I did not feel afraid, I felt comforted. I tried to be brave and asked in my mind, 'Is there someone really there or is it just my imagination?' Just then I felt as though someone were tugging at my skirt. I looked down at my skirt and to my surprise it was swaying very quickly as though someone had a hold of it and was moving it to and fro.

I sat there in amazement as my skirt swayed quite quickly. It then stopped for several minutes before swaying again. That afternoon I rang my friend Annette, who is also psychic, and told her about the skirt incident. As soon as I stopped talking Annette suddenly said, 'There is a man in spirit around you, Tash, and he's about thirty-two years old – that's the age he's showing me. His name is James Brooker and he looks like he's from the 1930s/1940s time period. I can tell this because of the type of clothes he's wearing.'

She told me he was wearing a waistcoat with a watch in one of the pockets. He had shiny black shoes and a cap on his head and he loved to go fishing. She also said that he was a very caring and kind man and did not mean me any harm. He was very gentle and tall, handsome and has brown hair.

She said that he has been lost and travelled a long way – he has been on a very long journey. He feels comfortable around me as I remind him of his wife. He is happy and settled here with me.

A few days later I was sweeping the floor in the living room when I looked up and saw a tall silhouette of a man walk through our kitchen and into the dining room before vanishing. I knew straight away that it was James. He also keeps blowing on the back of my neck to get my attention.

That same day I was working at my computer while listening to 'Earth Angel' by the Penguins (one of my favourite songs) when I heard a male voice humming along to the song right behind me and right near my ear – I could actually feel warm breath on my ear. Of course when I turned around I couldn't see anyone there and I was home alone. Now each time I play that song I can hear James humming along.

Not long after James was humming along to 'Earth Angel', I heard a soft tapping on our kitchen cupboard. The tapping started off quietly but got louder and louder. I went over to the cupboard and opened it but as soon as I did the tapping stopped and there was nothing strange in the cupboard. I shut the cupboard and sat down and a minute later the tapping started up again. This began happening regularly and still does to this day.

James has many ways of letting me know that he's around. Sometimes I'll be watching telly when I feel someone tickling my feet. Or I feel James's presence by my side. I always see him out of the corner of my eye, or walking up our stairs. I don't think there's a day that goes by where I do not feel his presence. Even now while typing this entry I've seen a small glowing yellow light ball move from above the computer to behind me and around me.

When I first met James I was going through very bad post-natal depression. I felt like giving up on life and I was at my lowest. Then James came along and helped to give me hope and love and support. Not long after meeting James I found a brilliant job at The Psychic Detective website. I also created Psychic Direct and other websites. I even started up a small group where we learnt all about spirit guides and angels. James helped me through some of the tough times in my life.

I am forever grateful to James for all the help and support he has offered me over the years. He is my hero and I am so grateful that he decided to stay with me and be my very own spirit guide. He helps me when I do my work and helps to guide me each day. I have a deep love for James – a brotherly love for my special spirit guide.

Natasha has more inspiring experiences to share in the pages below and on her free online psychic friends' website *psychicdevelopmentgroup.webs.com*, an online spiritual growth website. For her, the appearance of a departed friend who had died as a child wasn't frightening but rather it felt like they were two best friends back together again.

Roland

One night I was asleep in my bed when I suddenly awoke, feeling as if I was being watched. I could feel a heavy pressure at the end of my bed by my feet. I looked up and there was a boy aged about eighteen, the same age as myself at the time.

He was very handsome and was wearing a red swimsuit and had thick curly blond locks. I did not feel frightened of him and we spoke for what felt like hours. He said that he had drowned in our pool many years ago. I felt as though I had known him all my life.

It is only now that I have realized that the boy at my bed was a friend of mine who had passed away. I know that the spirit boy was Roland as he is one of my spirit guides and I talk to him now.

Whether or not we get to meet them or even sense them, I feel that we all have spirit guides around us who are ready and willing to help us in any way they can – we just need to ask! I do think that we can become more tuned in to the spirits around us, as I describe in the next chapter. We can develop our awareness and our senses and so pick up more easily on the signs they give us.

Again for Natasha, the appearance of a spirit when she was a little girl gave her great comfort when her pet dog had been taken ill.

Touched by a spirit

When I was seven years of age I sat outside on the porch with our pet dog who was very ill – he had tick bite fever. It was a crisp night and the moon shone brightly. I can remember it as though it was yesterday, I began to pray for our beloved pet and asked the Lord to watch over him and make him well.

I also asked for a sign that he would be okay. Just then I heard a woman's soft voice call out my name. I glanced up and to my surprise I saw a beautiful lady in a long dress to her ankles.

She had long hair down her back. She appeared as a misty, dim but glowing, monochrome figure but I could clearly make out her every feature. It is really hard to explain what I mean. She did not have wings like in the story-books but I knew at once that she was an angel.

Behind her was an open door in the exact same light as she was and again I could make out each feature of the door. She called out my name several more times and I can clearly remember being amazed that she knew what my name was. She then held her hand out towards the door and asked me to follow her.

Reality suddenly hit me as I realized that there was an angel standing before me. I do not know why I did what I did next but I leaped to my feet and ran as fast as I could into the house.

Suddenly I stopped and looked back to where she had been standing but she had gone. I ran and told my mother about what I had just witnessed and that I believed that our dog was dying and the angel was preparing me for what was about to happen.

I said that our dog would be happy and would be looked after by God and all the angels. My mother sent me to my room and told me to stop talking such rubbish. The next morning I was awoken by my mother. She held me close and told me that our pet dog had passed away in the night; she said that he was not suffering any more.

I looked up at her and sobbed my heart out, but although I was very upset and sad about our dog passing away, I felt happy as I knew he had gone to a better place and was being taken care of. To this day I still wonder who the angel was and what would have happened if I had followed her, and gone with her through that door.

Sometimes it amazes me how far and wide my books have travelled. When I received this letter all the way from Africa I could hardly believe it. It is so vivid in its descriptions, I felt transported. As with so many of the stories I am grateful to be sent, Val's grief and pain at losing her grandson are palpable, but she also shares with us moments of wonder.

A beautiful young lion

I have just finished your book *Celtic Angels*, the first of yours I have read. I live in Zambia and it isn't easy to find or buy books but I was drawn to this title when I spotted it on a supermarket shelf. It was the end of the month and so I was budget-shopping – anyway, let's just say we had stewing meat instead of rump that night!

I have had several experiences which I would like to share with you.

Some twenty years ago, our very much beloved grandson passed away from malaria at the age of six while we were having a holiday in the Zambezi Valley. The saddest thing was that he was staying with us at the time while his mother was working miles away. We were far away from the nearest hospital, and when we knew something was wrong we were unable to make it there in time; it was heart-breaking.

When my husband was returning to camp a few days later from the town we went to, he came across a beautiful young lion standing on a bank, just looking down on the car. Although there were known to be lions in the area, they were seldom seen as it was a busy road with trucks and lots of traffic. My husband felt amazed. Our youngest son and one of our workers were with him; they were all convinced it was our grandson come to say goodbye.

When my husband collected me a few days later, we encountered a whole pride of lions in almost the same spot, lying in the road; it was amazing and something we will never forget.

Many years later we had moved to South Africa, which we did not enjoy, and I was really depressed. Life was very difficult, my children were all either preparing to move to other continents or had already done so. Money was tight, our rented house had been sold, and I didn't know where to turn. I went to bed early, and called to my angels for comfort, then I lay on my stomach on the bed, close to tears. Then I had the most amazing feeling of soft wings caressing my back. There was a tremendous sense of peace and somehow my problems melted away, and I could face another day.

A year or so later, we were packing to return to Zambia, thanks to our wonderful daughter and son-in law (our angels), when my mother-in-law passed away. Unfortunately, we had been unable to visit when she was ill, due to money constraints and passport problems, and so my husband was very upset but we knew she would have understood, she was a kind woman. The day after we heard the news, we were going to work on our usual route, through a built-up area with busy traffic, when a beautiful antelope (a bushbuck) crossed the road in front of us, pausing to look straight at us before walking across the road. It was incredible – we knew there were such animals around but had never seen them in three years along that road. I knew it was Mom come to tell us she understood why we were not with her.

This year on the anniversary of our grandson's birthday, I picked some beautiful roses as I always do, both for him and for our son who passed away many years ago at just a year old. While I was arranging the two vases, I thought suddenly of my stillborn baby who we had lost over thirty-five years ago, something I had not thought about in years, and did a special vase for her as well. That night I had the most vivid dream, which I won't forget (and I forget my name at the drop of a hat) of a beautiful meadow full of flowers and a beautiful little girl, who I was rolling around with and laughing. It was surreal. Thank you, angels, for letting me know she is also around me.

Heaven on earth

Heaven has a way of appearing in the manner best suited to us as individuals, so while for some people that might be a seven-foot-tall angel with huge wings and a white robe, to others heaven will reveal itself through other humans. Often, heavenly helpers or angels will look like nurses, priests or monks. I've received many stories of a nurse dressed in an old-fashioned uniform suddenly appearing at the foot of the hospital bed, only to seemingly disappear into thin air minutes later. And there are the times when complete strangers somehow turn up to lend us a helping hand at exactly our moment of dire need. Sometimes they might simply be a human acting as an angel, sometimes I think they might be guided to our side through a bit of divine intervention.

The angels come to visit us, and we only know them when they are gone.

George Eliot

Michelle was in hospital when she had a surprise visit.

Who was that lady?

Hi Theresa, I've just finished reading your book, which was greatly uplifting, and it reminded me of a strange thing that happened to me.

I was in hospital after having a gallbladder removal operation in 2009. It was meant to be day surgery but I was told I would have to stay in for a night as other tests were needed. I was the only one left on the day ward, and ended up having to stay for a week because while running tests they could see I had a swollen bile duct and they were concerned that there might be a tumour present.

One day, after I had returned from another test to the private side room where they had moved me, a lady who looked about fifty years old knocked on my door. She said she was a volunteer for the hospital and would I mind if we prayed together. I said yes only because I would have felt terrible saying no to her, so there we were praying for my health amongst other things and after about ten or fifteen minutes we said goodbye. As she left, I immediately looked out of my door to see where she went but she had gone. It was a long straight corridor before you were able to turn so it was as though she had just disappeared. When I asked the nurse about her she told me no one had been on the ward as you have to buzz to get in, so I shuffled off before she thought I was crazy and didn't mention it again. Eventually, all my tests came back clear, and to this day I still wonder who that lady was and where she vanished to. This experience started me on my own path of spirituality and being open to the idea that maybe she was my guardian angel who had come to help me.

Solana's story is a simple and beautiful description of a moment shared.

A gift of comfort

I wish to share an amazing experience I had very recently. I am part way through reading your book *An Angel Healed Me*, which is excellent. My experience happened in a church just over a week ago. I was deep in prayer and was praying for various reasons. I had had a difficult week and was feeling upset due to a holiday I was supposed to be going on getting cancelled. Usually I would finish a prayer with the sign of the cross and leave. However, on this occasion I did something I've not done before. I asked for a sign that everything would be okay.

Almost immediately I became aware of a dark shadow out of my left eye. I turned my head and noticed a lady (I didn't see her face but just knew she was a lady) wearing dark old-fashioned-style clothing at my side. She reached her hand out towards mine and placed a set of rosary beads in my hand. As she did so she said, 'Here, take these.' I looked at the set of rosary beads in my hand and then looked up at her to thank her but she had disappeared. I did not hear any footsteps. I was sitting by the church doors and did not hear the sound of the doors open or close. This lady just seemed to come out of nowhere and then disappear again. I felt very comforted by this strange experience.

Sometimes, heavenly helpers use pretty imaginative ways to help us out, as I discovered when I read Julie's letter.

Finish your cigarette

I am nearly at the end of your book *Angel Babies* and I felt inspired to tell you my story.

It happened one rainy dark evening a few years ago. I had had a horrible row with my boyfriend and stormed out of the house. While waiting for the bus to my mum's (where else does a girl go when she's in trouble and upset?) I realized I had run out of cigarettes. Feeling very upset, for I loved and still love my partner very much, I burst out crying. There was a shop just across the road from the bus stop but I felt silly to go into the shop crying.

I had not noticed an elderly gentleman sitting next to me who now asked me what the matter was. I briefly told him my tale of woe and explained my need for a cigarette. He immediately offered me one, which I gratefully took, but then I said that I should still pop into the shop in any case. He stressed for me to finish my cigarette first and go after. Just at that moment a car came hurtling down the road at break-neck speed and crashed into a wall, spinning over onto its side. If I had started walking across the road to the shop the car would have hit me for sure.

The bus came moments later and I turned to the man, but he was nowhere to be seen. As I sat on the bus I scanned outside but he was gone. Could this have been my angel?

Whether the man in the bus shelter was simply a kind stranger or a spirit guide, he was a messenger from heaven either way.

It's funny how often there will be an odd detail that stands out and gives us a big clue that our celestial guides are at work. When heavenly guides appear as nurses they will often get the era a bit wrong and look quite old-fashioned, like our childhood clichéd image of a nurse. When Barbara met her spirit guide, he looked very smart and handsome, but brought a 'friend' with him who stood out like a sore thumb!

Dancing with heaven

A number of years ago I had an experience that I have always wandered about. At the time my husband and I had divorced and I was on a night out with a friend at a rock 'n' roll club near to my home.

I had been dancing with my friend and it was my turn to go to the bar for drinks. As I was standing there at the bar a very smart gentleman asked me if he could buy me a drink. I thanked him but declined as I had just bought one. He had a very nice suit, white shirt and tie and I couldn't take my eyes off him because he was the smartest man in the room, and he was also very handsome. But what I thought was strange was that he had a young man with him who was dressed so differently, in a very dated royal blue suit and a flowery shirt with wide lapels. He was a bit on the scruffy side. He didn't speak but walked slightly behind the other gentleman at all times.

After a while the smart man came to me with a drink and asked if I still drank brandy and Coke; how did he know I used to drink that but hadn't for years? He asked me to dance with him and was a good dancer; as we talked he seemed to know quite a bit about me and I didn't know how as we had never met. He then told me he would always look after me as he was my guardian angel and he was called Gabriel. I was a bit shocked but actually believed him.

After we finished dancing I went over to my friend; she asked where I had been as she had been looking for me for half an hour, although during this time I had been on the dance floor right next to her. She didn't believe me when I told her as the man was nowhere to be seen – he and his friend had both disappeared. When I spoke to other people I knew in the club it turned out no one had seen either of them. I found this hard to believe as the man's friend stood out like a sore thumb in his old-fashioned clothes – he was someone you couldn't help but look at.

I have never forgotten this experience. Sometimes I wonder if I imagined it, but I know it really happened and that I am blessed to have met my guardian angel.

In Ruby's story, not only did she have a premonition of her father's illness in a dream, but there is also the appearance of a messenger. Again, she'll never know if he was simply someone in the right place at the right time or if he was a spirit taking on human form to make sure they got the message to go to her mum's side.

The messenger

Right after my daughter was born in 1958 I started having dreams about someone stabbing my father in the back and the chest. For some reason they were in black and white, when all my other dreams had been in vivid colour. This same dream persisted for three nights.

My daughter was eighteen months old and as usual we had travelled up to my parents for Christmas Day. When we arrived all was quiet and my mother was cooking Christmas dinner. Mum sat us down and told us that Dad had suffered a heart attack. The doctor said it was coronary thrombosis and that Dad was unlikely to last until the morning.

When my eldest sister arrived we sat together at the side of Dad's bed, and I remember telling her not to worry, that he was not going to die yet as his time hadn't come. I don't know why I said this; it came straight out of the blue. She just looked at me without saying a word, and as it turned out, I was right.

Three years later a man came into my husband's place of work, walked straight up to my husband and asked if he knew that his father-in-law had been taken very ill. My husband John didn't hesitate but came straight home and took me and our two children up to Mum's. She wasn't there but a kind neighbour told us that my father had just been taken by ambulance to the hospital as he had had a heart attack. Sadly when I rang the hospital they told us that my father had died ten minutes earlier.

We never did find out who it was who brought the message to my husband's place of work as no one knew him and no one saw him leave.

Sometimes it is surprising just who has a story about heaven – the people you might least expect to talk about something like divine intervention surprise you with their candour and openness. While helping me with this book, Kate was chatting to a group of family and friends about it and her father Vince immediately said, 'You remember my story, it was in Italy, with that pack of dogs.' Here's his story:

A Tuscan angel

My wife Lin and I were on a walking tour in Tuscany some years ago when on our final leg of an amazing journey we had a life-threatening experience and it's always been my belief that St Francis of Assisi was looking over us.

The last day of the walk was from Spello, a wonderful Italian hilltop town, to Assisi, taking a route that went straight up and over Mount Subasio, an imposing local landmark rising to over 600 metres above sea level.

We set off on a beautiful autumn Italian day in bright sunshine and made a good pace, reaching the summit of Subasio in less than two hours. From here you can see Assisi nestling in the valley below and after a traverse across meadows at the top of Subasio you then wind your way down into the town itself.

We could see across the meadows sheep grazing on the hillside and began a path towards them. We were enjoying the views, the weather and the freedom when suddenly almost out of nowhere there came a pack of five howling Pyrenean mountain dogs bearing down on us very quickly. Lin and I became really scared as the lead dog ran at us. As he and the others got closer I decided to be a hundred per cent passive and stopped walking and let my hands hang down loosely and told Lin to do the same. The lead dog was now yards away and my first thoughts were that this was going to be very painful as its nose almost touched my arm.

Within seconds I came out of my trance and realized that he and the other dogs had not attacked but were now growling and circling me while, as I looked up, I saw Lin moving slowly away to a safer area.

I summoned up my strength and began to berate the dogs and call for help from the shepherd, who was nowhere to be seen, but it appeared to do the trick. The dogs began to lose interest – I was no threat – and I began to edge carefully away down the meadow to meet up with Lin. Very shaken but extremely relieved, we got to the end of the meadow and took the famous path that St Francis had trodden centuries before and made our wonderful descent into Assisi.

St Francis had been with us every step of the way and then it transpired I had another chance to feel that spirit.

It came the next day. Lin loves old buildings and churches

and so wanted to explore Assisi. I on the other hand prefer the outdoors and decided to take a walk some twenty miles out of the town to another hilltop town and get the bus back.

Most of the walk was along an old and famous via bianca that went through spectacular Italian countryside. Mile after mile up and up through hills as far as the eye could see I walked with no sign of people, cars or even grazing animals until after approximately fifteen miles I saw ahead something that was really frightening. Sheep grazing to the right and on the path some half a mile in front of me a group of dogs in front of an old red car and seemingly no shepherd.

What should I do, could I traverse either to the right or left and give the dogs a wide berth? I was thinking what an extra long walk it would be to turn back now when, hallelujah, along the via behind me appeared an old grey Fiat car. I stepped into its path and waved to the driver who pulled up and said, 'Salute' and in very broken Italian I explained the situation. He said get in and off we went, past the dogs and he dropped me off on the via about half a mile further on.

Relief was enormous and again I am sure St Francis was there at that very moment. I walked into the town, had a coffee and caught the next bus back to Assisi.

I am not a religious person but whenever I travel and am near a church of St Francis of Assisi I go and say hello and make a little vow of thanks.

Teresa also felt like she had been saved by Earth Angels while on holiday in Italy.

Saved by the hairdresser!

In autumn 2005, we booked an Agroturismo farmhouse holiday in Le Marche, Italy. I had made the booking online as we really needed a complete break away as we were both experiencing a great deal of stress through work and family problems.

Everything was in a rush. When we arrived at Ancona airport I searched in my bag for the details of our accommodation and realized to my horror that I had left them by the computer at home. I felt sick to my stomach as we had no address, nor the name of the people or any telephone number with which to contact them. All we knew was the first name of the owner of the farmhouse. It was late afternoon and I had no idea how we were going to find the place as we drove round and round in circles, up and down hills, looking for someone we could ask. Everywhere was deserted. Finally, we came to an old town called Cupramontana. Our only chance was to ask someone if they knew of the farmhouse, a long shot at best. By then, it was 4.30 and the light was fading. We were very stressed. We asked a couple of old men sitting outside a café but they spoke in dialect and shook their heads. We asked a woman and another man in the street but no one knew. We knew that once it got dark there would be no way we would find the Agroturismo and might have to sleep in the hire car. Even our mobile phone didn't work in Italy. We were truly stuck.

Then as we stood not knowing what to do next we

spotted a young man in a brilliant white T-shirt and black trousers walking towards us down the middle of the street. I summoned up the courage and in my best broken Italian asked him if he knew the man who owned the house by just his first name. Yes! He knew exactly who we meant and exactly where we needed to go. He said he cut the owner's hair. He didn't have a car but went off for a few minutes and came back with a friend in his car; we then followed them through a few miles of winding lanes until they pointed down a track and told us it's that way. We thanked them, and they were gone.

Perhaps it was just luck, but we felt saved from a very difficult situation that night.

This story reminds me that one of the most powerful ways to bring the light of heaven to earth is to be heavenly yourself in your interactions with others. I do believe that heavenly helpers themselves sometimes appear to us in the guise of humans, and I also believe that we are also drawn to the people who are meant to be spiritual companions in life. Remember that the language of heaven is one of love; so when we offer comfort, encouragement or support to others we are drawing on the same energy as celestial beings – we are talking in their language.

Irene learned from her own healing experience that she too could offer help to others.

Never alone

As I was growing up I always felt someone was with me, but I have had my struggles. I had three miscarriages, which I took hard, and then had two sons. The younger son proved a real worry and problem to me through his teenage years. I was so concerned that I became quite ill. Then by chance (or was it?), one day I bumped into an old friend who suggested I go to the local spiritualist church for a healing. I wasn't very keen but decided to go, thinking I had nothing to lose as conventional medicine hadn't proved successful for me.

The healing didn't cure all my ills, but it did help to calm me down and made me begin to look at things differently, to deal with things better. My healer was a lovely man called John who helped me overcome my fears and tears until I felt well again (I feel he was an 'Earth Angel').

In a way this is just where my story starts as I then became a healer myself. I work in the local area helping people in whatever way I can, putting something back into life as I felt very blessed in mine. My son came right and is doing well, and between both of my sons I have five grandchildren, who I am lucky enough to help look after. With limited time on my hands now, I work at home offering healing, relaxation and meditation classes to those like me who sometimes need a helping hand or for someone to be there for them.

I know I am helped by angels; sometimes I see them but

I know they are always there. They are a source of confidence and positivity, as well as calm and peace, and they make sure that I never feel alone.

For those who connect with spirit – whether in heaven, on earth or within themselves – life is never the same again because they understand that the meaning and purpose of their lives is to love. And by a wonderful act of synchronicity – which I always think is the language heaven speaks – the simple but life-changing message that love is life came through loud and clear to Kate as she worked tirelessly on this book. Here is her heartfelt story:

A note from Kate

Like Theresa, I've been involved in publishing books from the beginning of my career. It's a bit of a surprise our paths haven't fully crossed one another before as my second job was with a spiritual publisher called Element Books. I don't have any psychically gifted members of my family but my parents have always been very open about spiritual things, rather than religious. My mum is very intuitive and always picking up the phone just as the person she was about to call calls her. I didn't think my dad would be all that responsive when I said I was helping with a book on angels, when he proceeded to recount to me an experience he and Mum had in Italy one year when he was convinced they were protected by a guardian angel when confronted by a pack of vicious dogs. It's been included in this chapter.

For my own part, although I've been interested in spiritual books for many years, as well as more general health and wellbeing books, I've never really thought about such things as guardian angels or messages from heaven. But as I've been helping out with compiling the amazing and always touching stories within these pages, I have been thinking about some of the wonderful coincidences in my own life, how my friends truly are my collection of angels and how I have definitely felt a helping hand at times in my life.

The biggest message I take from all of stories that Theresa has collected over the years and shared in her books is that love is the most important thing in this life.

I spent most of my life in the proverbial closet; by my mid-thirties I had hardly had a proper relationship and when I decided to leave my job as a publisher and become a freelance writer I also decided that it was about time I just took a big gulp and told everyone that I liked women.

Well, I didn't manage to surprise one person! For a moment I did regret that it had taken so long to come out, but this didn't last long because by being honest with everyone I had connected with myself, perhaps even with my inner angel, and suddenly I went from being invisible and never being asked out to being noticed, by men and women alike. This was great, except that emotionally I had about the same maturity as a teenager, and so I ended up behaving similarly.

I ended up having a rather awkward affair with a girl who was living with her girlfriend. My friends were sweet – they didn't want to burst my bubble, my having just come out, –

but they tried their best to gently help me see that it wasn't the best idea, all to no avail.

One evening, I was set to go and meet her. I was with a couple of close friends beforehand; we met for a drink in a pub but then just as we were leaving my friend looked down for her handbag and exclaimed that it had been taken. It had literally happened in the last few minutes and we couldn't believe how someone had managed to get under the table without us noticing. She was really upset but I thought she took it incredibly well – her house keys, driving licence and all her credit cards were in the bag, which was also very expensive itself. We went to the police station and the other friend and I waited for an hour while she gave a statement.

The first thing my friend said when she came out of the police station was, 'Well, Kate, I think my angels were looking out for you tonight! You'll never get to the club now.' It was typical of her to see a silver lining despite her own loss. We all burst out laughing, and she was right, that night took the wind completely out of the affair and also reminded me there are angels right here in our everyday lives, we only have to look to our friends to see them.

But here is the best part of the story. It was nearly Christmas and I was invited to a shaman ceremony by a good friend. I'd never been to one before and she said to prepare a song for the ceremony, something that had significance for me or for the year ahead. I'm a terrible singer and so I was really nervous but I seemed to know immediately what song I had to sing. Here is the chorus, it's by a folk singer called Edie Brickell.

'I'm glad no one's here, just me by the sea
I'm glad no one's here, to mess it up for me
I'm glad no one's here, just me by the sea
But man I wish I had a hand to hold.'

You see, I'm so independent and quite happy in my own company, but my heart and my soul knew it was about time to fall in love! Well, a month later I met Nicole, or I should say Nicole found me, and by the spring my friends were pulling me aside to whisper firmly in my ear, 'Don't you let go of her.' I don't know who was listening when I sang that song, but thank you.

Spreading your wings

In the next chapter we will explore how we can talk to heaven, how to open up our hearts to the possibility of connection, how to develop our intuition and our senses so that we might hear the whisper of an angel or feel their touch on our cheek. In the same way, I hope that as we become more in tune with the piece of heaven that lives inside all of us, we will become more sensitive to the needs of those around us, so that we can be there at the right time and offer a hand to hold, a listening ear or a shoulder to cry on. In this way others can catch a glimpse of heaven through us.

If we were all like angels, the world would be a heavenly place.

Anonymous

CHAPTER SIX

Talking to heaven

How wonderful it must be to speak the language of heaven
– with no words for hate and a million words for love.

Eileen Elias Freeman

W hen people think of communicating with heaven, with their departed loved ones or their spirit guides, they might think first of mediums; that you would need the help of a person with special abilities to be able to make any kind of contact. I will discuss the pros and cons of mediums in a moment, but first I would like to emphasize that there is a great deal we can do ourselves in gentle ways to encourage our own individual conversations with heaven. When we open our hearts and then our minds, and when we practise tuning into our thoughts, emotions and senses, then we open ourselves to the potential of seeing, hearing or sensing messages from heaven. Perhaps we feel a guiding hand, or receive a visit in our dreams, as I have experienced myself. We might even ask directly for help or find comfort in passing on our own messages of love. In this chapter, I will explore how these things are possible and how we might take steps ourselves to open up the lines of communication in the way that best suits us, whether that might be through prayer, or developing our intuition or our awareness of our physical senses such as hearing and touch.

Mediums

The movie *Ghost* may be entertaining but it sustains the misguided idea that communicating to the world of spirit is a specialist job. There is a place for mediums but often too much opportunity for fraud and cold reading.

There are a number of ways you might look for and find a good medium. The most popular way is through referral or word of mouth. A friend or relative has had a positive experience and so you feel more confident about giving it a try yourself. This is the same with any kind of service, whether you are looking for a good dentist or a good accountant!

You might find it useful to go along to a medium demonstration in a small group, rather than immediately trying a one-to-one session. Really check whether the medium makes you feel comfortable and is someone you feel you could make a connection with. Psychic circles are similar in that you attend in a group setting so you can get a feel for the process.

You might hear a medium on the radio or research one on the internet, especially if none of your friends and family have been to see a medium or feel they would recommend someone. Check their online referrals carefully and also listen to your own intuition when you meet them for the first time. This can be tricky as you want to be as open and receptive as possible while also being aware of the potential for fraud in these situations. That's why it can be so helpful to either be introduced by a friend if at all possible or go along to a group demonstration or class first to see how you feel about this person.

Some people find spiritualist churches supportive and a way to get to know a medium before requesting a personal reading. Again, the group setting can be very helpful in the early stages of deciding if you want to ask for a medium's help.

If you do go ahead and make an appointment with a medium, make sure you don't pass on any significant information about yourself or those you wish to communicate with. Even during the reading don't react strongly to anything you hear if that's possible. The medium should offer a piece of information that makes you feel sure they have made contact, like a nickname, a very specific object or message. Of course, it might not be possible to make contact at the exact time of your meeting and through this particular medium, so don't be despondent if it's not the right time.

While mediums can be helpful to some people, I always recommend direct communication – a personal relationship – with heaven but first there must be a time for grief.

Travelling through grief

Heaven knows we need never be ashamed of our tears, for they are rain upon the blinding dust of earth, over-lying our hard hearts. I was better after I had cried, than before – more sorry, more aware of my own ingrat-itude, more gentle.

Charles Dickens, *Great Expectations*

When someone you love very much dies it can be devastating. The pain can be unbearable, as can any leftover regrets about whether there was any more you could have said or done. Grief is a process you need to work through before you can enter into a new and stronger relationship with that person in spirit, and the advice in this chapter can be used as a guide.

You may wish more than anything for a sign or a message from your loved one, but it's essential to take care of your grief and not get stuck in the intense pain you might be feeling. Even if we do experience contact with a departed loved one, this will never bring them back and so we need to reach a point where we can accept death and begin to come to terms with our loss. It is then that the channels of communication might be more open, rather than blocked by pain or anger.

The first step in grieving is to actually let yourself feel the grief, rather than be scared of it or put up a wall between you and your pain. Shock and then denial are the most common early responses to loss and it is denial that stops us from mourning, from even starting the healing process. If we become too attached to the idea of making contact with the spirit of the departed then we haven't really accepted they have gone – we are hanging on too tightly. We are protecting ourselves from the raw pain that comes once the numb shock has worn off, but it is a false protection, a delaying tactic. Denial also protects us from the confusing emotions like anger, guilt and helplessness that we feel after losing a loved one. We might be frightened by these emotions or not want to admit they are there, but allowing ourselves to fully experience them is essential. It is important not to push them down, where they may feed a depression, or outwards in the form of hurting or alienating others. Grief counselling can be extremely helpful if it is hard to navigate through any of these natural stages alone. Talking with friends and family is also all part of the healing – sharing memories, tears and laughter together.

Taking care of yourself through the process of grieving will help to keep you healthy in body, mind and spirit. Eating well, exercising and getting out into the natural world are all tonics during this time. And it is a process that has no fixed time-frame – every person experiences grief individually and some will move through to a positive place of acceptance and healing more quickly than others. It is important that people go at the pace which is right for them, but it is also important to keep taking gentle steps forward, however small.

The five stages of grief

It was Elisabeth Kübler-Ross who named the stages of grief as:

- Denial
- Anger
- Bargaining
- Depression
- Acceptance.

I think it is helpful for each of our own journeys to have a sense of what these stages are. Every single person has their own individual relationship with both life and death, so none of these stages are set in stone or always come in the same order. As Kübler-Ross herself said, you can't 'tuck messy emotions into neat packages'; but perhaps it can be helpful to think about the fact that we are all in the same boat in that we have all either lost or will lose someone who is very close to us.

Denial: The kind of denial Kübler-Ross was talking about is the feeling you just can't shake that your loved one might walk in the door at any moment, right as rain. This is like being in shock – the actual emotions of grief seem distant and as if they belong to somebody else. It is as though your mind or your body is protecting you from the pain of the reality through fear it will be just too much to cope with. It may be that your mind then allows the reality to sink in gradually, rather than in a big wave, so that you can begin to heal.

Anger: The anger people feel in their grief isn't usually very logical; it doesn't often make very much sense but in some ways it makes perfect sense, because it is in death that we realize we aren't in control. We wrestle with the thoughts that *there must have been something we could have done, it wasn't their time, how could this happen to such a good person, it isn't fair.* And at the same time as that anger tends to come to the surface, many of the other emotions associated with grief come rising up too, including our sadness and our pain. This is our mind's way of telling us that we have the strength to cope with these emotions now, although we might not realize that straight away.

Bargaining: This stage is closely associated with guilt, as we get stuck in a mental rut of thoughts that start with 'if only . . .' or 'what if . . .' These thoughts prevent us from moving towards any sense of acceptance about our loss and they can make us feel awful about ourselves – 'if only we had spent more time with them'. At this point we are stuck in the past like a broken record playing things over and over again.

Depression: The stage of depression brings us into the present, but for some of us the stark reality of loss is very cold and very lonely. It's hard to keep going, we struggle to find the will or the energy to get out of bed in the morning. What Kübler-Ross reminds us is that losing a loved one is depressing, it's okay to feel paralysed or want to withdraw, and that all of these feelings are natural. It is at this point that 'loss fully settles in your soul.' Kübler-Ross suggests that we see depression as a visitor, a part of the healing process that we needn't run away from, but that we can fully experience so that we may allow it to pass. For me, I know that hitting rock bottom was intensely painful, but it also meant that I gradually came up to the surface of my life again.

Acceptance: This stage is about accepting the reality that our loved one has passed, rather than saying that we are now 'okay' about it. We never have to be okay about losing someone, but we can accept it and learn to live with it. With healing, the chance for a new relationship comes – we allow ourselves to become close with the person again, to think of them, to hold them in our hearts.

Sometimes we feel as though we are meant to try and put a brave face on our grief or 'get back to normal', but the reality is that something has changed in our life, and it will never be quite the same again. The question and challenge is then what we decide to do with that change, whether we can find a way to be positive in this new life. A friend of mine lost her mother to cancer as a young teenager and then her best friend to the same disease in her early thirties. She was completely devastated and took a very long time to come to terms with her grief, but as she did she realized she had two of the most amazing spiritual guides one person could hope for. She knew her best friend would want her to take life by both hands and truly go for it, and gradually she did just that.

The same realization came to me some time after my mother died. At first I couldn't come to terms with the loss, but as I did I at last became truly open to the world of spirit. I knew that although my mother had died, my love for her was still as strong – it was a message in itself. I also knew that this love still went both ways, just like a conversation. My mother's love was still there for me in spirit, giving me comfort and strength and keeping a watchful eye over me.

Getting in touch: How to see, hear and sense spirit

Anyone can communicate with the spirit world, even if it seems some people have a more direct line than others. If you would like to learn how to feel, see and hear divine messages then this chapter will give you lots of practical advice that will help your fine-tuning. Many people will try communicating through a medium or psychic before they have tried to make contact themselves. I think it is different for everyone, so go with whichever way is comfortable for you, when it feels the right time. But I would say that simply chatting directly and personally to our angels or to the spirits of those we have loved and lost and asking questions is a great first step. And by chatting, I don't mean talking to yourself out loud, I mean a conversation within your mind and your heart. Talking to heaven in this way is often a support and comfort in itself, and sometimes brings a few interesting surprises. The answers may not come immediately but the more you keep thinking and asking within yourself, the more likely you are to get the answers you are seeking. Vitally important though is that you know what you are asking. Conversations are, after all, a two-way street.

Often, we assume that spirits will just suddenly appear with a message, but wouldn't it be easier for them if they knew what we were asking? Do you want a sign from above that you are not alone or do you have a specific question?

There are a few different ways in which we can begin to tune into heaven and start making contact or communicating. The key is to explore and to find a way that feels right to you.

The first thing is to consider why you want to make contact; do you need help with healing, for example, or have unanswered questions that you would very much like to ask? If we are feeling very lonely or struggling to cope with life, this is when we most need to let heaven know that we need help and support.

Try to concentrate on taking good care of yourself and your body. If you can practise reminding yourself of the preciousness of life, nature and the world we live in, then you will begin to nourish fertile ground in your feelings and your mind for making a connection. If you cling on to your frustrations or your tensions and anxieties, then your mind will automatically feel tighter, with less space in which wonderful things might take place. When we live, feel and breathe with respect for ourselves and all others, we create an openness that is friendly and inviting to souls both here in our world and perhaps beyond too.

The best remedy for those who are afraid, lonely or unhappy is to go outside, somewhere where they can be quite alone with the heavens, nature and God. Because only then does one feel that all is as it should be and

> *that God wishes to see people happy, amidst the simple*
> *beauty of nature. As long as this exists, and it certainly*
> *always will, I know that then there will always be com-*
> *fort for every sorrow, whatever the circumstances may*
> *be. And I firmly believe that nature brings solace in all*
> *troubles.*
>
> Anne Frank, *The Diary of a Young Girl*

To begin, you might simply start by asking for a bit of advice or help. As you do this, it can be helpful to visualize a warm, energizing light flowing over your body or entering your heart and mind. There are many ways to receive contact in return – actually hearing divine voices is just one, which is called clairaudience. Here are some of the others:

Clairvoyance: the ability to see either spirits themselves or in the forms of clouds, colours or bright lights. They might appear in your thoughts or your dreams, or not appear themselves but in a visual form of the information they wish to impart to you.

Clairaudience: this is where you might hear a voice, either in your mind or as if someone is standing near you, and includes messages that come through music or hearing your name being called and knowing the voice is from beyond this world.

Clairsentience: sometimes we may be able to sense contact, which can be felt through our emotions or through our senses of touch and smell in particular. For example, the smell of lavender or roses that suddenly wafts around us when there are no flowers to be seen, or a sudden sensation of being touched, or tapped on the shoulder, but when we look around, no one is there.

Claircognizance: on occasion we feel like we've had a flash of divine inspiration, when the perfect thought or idea has struck us just when we needed it, even though we were clueless until then that we even needed the thought. It feels like someone is looking out for us today.

Calling heaven

As you begin to practise talking to heaven, try to be as specific as possible. If you have been struggling to come to terms with the grief process, ask for comfort and the knowledge that things are okay. Spirits make excellent guides, so if you would like some help finding the right therapy or treatment, or you need help with a decision, then go ahead and ask. What is it that you want to heal? What do you want to let go of? Be open to the answers, release any fears or doubts you might have and just allow yourself to be receptive and welcoming. I'm not sure what it is about the human psyche but sometimes we seem to be more comfortable with negative thoughts and with our hurts than with opening ourselves up to all the incredible opportunities in our lives. It takes a leap of faith to let go of these weights and free our minds but when we do the dreams in our hearts can become a reality.

You might want to make contact so that you can help someone who is close to you; they might be sick and in need of healing comfort or be at a crisis point in their life so in great need of some positive guidance. Simply by praying to heaven and sending out our good wishes to our loved ones we are having the best conversation of all. In many religious traditions the main role of many holy men and women is to spend as much time as possible in prayer, literally flooding the world with positive thoughts and energy. Zen monks will travel to Auschwitz to the site of concentration camps and sit for days, gradually cancelling out some of the terrible negative energy of the place with their prayers and their tears.

Signs

It's an obvious thing to say, but in order to hear a message, you need to be listening. You need to open up all of your senses and be on the lookout. I've included some of the signs you might be given as a means of contact to give you an idea of the ways in which this might happen. There is no definitive list, but these are some of the common cues:

- There might be particular objects, songs or symbols that have always connected you with a loved one and that appear almost as if out of nowhere.
- The sensation that someone has touched you, brushed your cheek, put an arm around you or kissed you, when no one is there. Or you might hear your voice called out of nowhere.
- A feeling that rushes down your spine.
- You might notice a movement in your peripheral vision or hear a soft, gentle ringing like a hum in your ear.
- Smell is a wonderful sense through which contact might

come, especially the comforting scent of a loved one's perfume that has no explainable source but surrounds us like a hug.

- It might feel as though you are dreaming more and the dreams are more vivid and memorable, as if the dial has been turned up a notch.

- If you have asked for a sign you might see something like pristine white feathers where they shouldn't be, butterflies turning up completely out of the blue, or perhaps clouds with formations that seem to reveal something to you.

- If you have asked for help, you may experience an amazing coincidence or discover that a problem rights itself in a way that you can't really explain. Or you might simply sense a supportive presence or have a sudden feeling of pure joy, happiness or clarity just when you really need it.

The quieter you become, the more you can hear.
Ram Dass

Making contact with the afterlife might not be quite as direct as a phone call – often the messages we receive are very faint and there might be a great deal of interference on the line. Don't be afraid to open up the connection and start the conversation yourself. You might find that loved ones deliberately give you the space needed to grieve and heal without their presence getting in the way, but if the time is right and you are tuned in then you might begin to see, feel, hear or sense the signs.

You can begin to develop your sensitivity, especially if you recognize that you lean towards a particular sense; if for example you are a very visual person, or a great listener, or perhaps you have a strong gut instinct and sense things from within. On a practical level, it is a good idea to keep a journal of your thoughts, emotions, dreams and experiences. You may also wish to write down your questions in your journal, or even write a letter to a loved one. Again, it all depends on what feels right to you. Keeping a dream journal in particular can be very helpful as we tend to forget most of our dreams very quickly after waking. The more you write them down as soon as you awake, the more familiar you will become with them and you will be able to notice the difference between an everyday dream and a dream message or contact. As I will explore more in Chapter Seven, when readers describe psychic dreams to me they are always struck by how vivid and real they were, and how these dreams will stay with a person for many years while all others quickly fade away.

> *Miracles . . . seem to me to rest not so much upon faces or voices or healing power coming suddenly near to us from afar off, but upon our perceptions being made finer, so that for a moment our eyes can see and our ears can hear what is there about us always.*
>
> Willa Cather

Here are some other ways to help tune in:

- Pay attention to your emotions – as with all communication in our lives, it is truly meaningful when we are really in touch with our own emotions, when we are genuine and open. Especially when we are grieving it is easy to end up pushing our painful emotions down beneath the surface because they feel too raw to deal with, and we worry that we won't be able to cope with them. The trouble is that when we do that, those difficult emotions can become like walls or barriers to our true self and in turn become a barrier between us and making a connection with the afterlife. Start to recognize your emotions as you go through your day. Let them come, even if they are difficult, because as you let them come you will also be able to let them go.

- Pay attention to your thoughts – our thoughts are often a bit of a whirlwind, wandering about all over the place; and then suddenly, like a bolt out of the blue, we know what to do. By going through your daily activities with an increased sense of mindfulness, so that you are gradually a little more aware of your thoughts as they come and go, then you will help to clear the static on the frequency of your mind. It is easy to be wary of our thoughts as we know they are often the source of our anxiety. But if we can become more familiar with our minds then they will tend to become calmer and more open, both helpful for tuning into communication, whether earthly or heavenly.

- Practise empathy – when we empathize with another person, we are able to mentally and emotionally put ourselves into their shoes and see things from their perspective. We let go of our own agenda and become much better at truly listening.

We become open to noticing the vibe of another person. We know how they feel. Empathy is a wonderful emotional skill to be able to develop, especially when it comes to the art of conversation, which is really what heavenly communication is all about.

- Open your heart – as you become more aware of your emotions and your thoughts and you develop your capacity for empathy, you will automatically be going a long way to opening up your heart to the possibility of communicating with heaven or the divine in some way. Let go of any niggling doubts and please don't be at all frightened at the thought of being contacted as everything sent to you from heaven is positive, supportive and loving. Let go of any 'what ifs' and open up to 'why not?'

- Be sensitive to touch – it is easy to take our sense of touch for granted and not realize just how much information we take in about the world as we touch, feel and hold objects, textures and, of course, each other. Being sensitive to human touch will in turn help to keep our heart open and heighten our ability to *feel* things that are not of this world. Touch is a wonderful form of communication: think about how we are able to read another person through their eyes, their body language and even a handshake. With touch we are able to say things that we can't put into words, things that are beyond words. The same is true for our spiritual guides. They may not always be able to come to us with definitive answers, but as they brush our cheek or kiss our forehead their love and support come shining through.

- Take care of yourself – just as negative emotions can build up barriers between ourselves and our ability to make contact with the other side, the same is true when we don't look after our health. Eating well and enjoying movement are an incredibly positive choice we can make that increases our sense of self-worth and our belief. With a healthy mind and body we will really begin to open up all the available channels for communication.

- Get back to nature – many heavenly signs come in the forms of nature, from birds and butterflies turning up in the strangest places to incredible cloud formations, so if you can become closer to nature you might find yourself becoming closer to spirit. Especially when we live in towns and cities, it is easy to feel separate from nature, and yet it is nature that provides us with everything we need to survive and flourish, from the air we breathe, to the food we eat and the shelter above our heads. If you can develop your connection with nature, you will develop your awareness of life in general. Listen to the birds, the dawn chorus on a warm spring morning is about as heavenly a sound as there exists on earth.

- Go cloud-watching – you might see a feather, wings or even an angel shape or face when you look up at the sky. This is one of my favourite personal experiences; I remember years ago when I was feeling very sad one particular day thinking about my late mother and how she hadn't known her grandchildren, my children. It was such a beautiful day with a crisp, bright blue sky; one moment I was shielding my eyes from the glare of the winter sun and the next moment I opened them to see one solitary cloud in the sky, amazingly in the perfect form of an angel with wings, a gown and gently folded hands. It was the first time I had ever seen such a thing and I felt so grateful. I was filled with a sense of comfort and peace and knew my mother wasn't so far away after all.

A man on the street is pointing up to the sky. 'Look, an angel,' he yells. Passers-by laugh. 'You fool, that is only a cloud.' How wonderful it would be to see angels where there are only clouds. How sad it would be to see only clouds where there are angels.

Anonymous

First thing in the morning and last thing at night

I think it is a very good idea to spend just a few moments when you wake in the morning and before you go to sleep at night thinking about heaven, using that peaceful time to ask questions or simply let loved ones in spirit know how you are doing. Creating a little time and space for this type of contemplation will help to open up your heart and invite heavenly communication to come your way. And whether you receive direct contact immediately or it takes a bit of time, all of the ideas in this chapter will also help you to be in touch with yourself and your emotions, and this heightened sensitivity will help you to empathize with others, enjoy the beauty of nature, embrace a lifestyle to take care of your health and even develop feelings of confidence.

If you want to have a conversation with heaven, then don't be afraid to just start. The piece of heaven inside of you will always be listening.

CHAPTER SEVEN

Following the light

The grass he walked through was new and a sweet smell clung to his clothes. There was blue dye on his hands from the wild irises . . . that the colour of the sky was a shade that could never be replicated in any photograph, just as Heaven could never be seen from the confines of Earth.

Alice Hoffman, *The River King*

What do all the stories in this book share? To me, they share a sense of trust in something we may not be able to see or touch every day but that we can feel if only we let ourselves. In addition, these stories share beauty, love and healing. For the individuals who wrote down their experiences they have often provided a moment of huge spiritual growth, and I also very often feel their sense of relief and happiness that there are so many people who are willing to listen to and read their story with an open heart and mind. Perhaps even as you read the stories you may be touched by them and detect a continued spiritual awakening in yourself. Or they may be simply fascinating to read, an exploration of how we as humans make connections that are beyond our physical realm, not just with the afterlife but with each other, with nature, and with ourselves.

What are now commonly known as near-death experiences provide us with the best evidence for communication with the departed and the most convincing proof we have that heaven is real and that we can have a strong connection to it on earth. Whether from films and books, or reading about others' accounts, or through a friend or loved one who had their own near-death experience, we are used to hearing phrases like 'my whole life flashed before me' or 'I was walking through a tunnel' or 'he told me to go back, that it wasn't my time yet.'

People who have either been clinically dead and then brought back to life, or who were on the brink of death but were saved at the last moment, occasionally return with some of the most incredible descriptions of the afterlife – some may even have had a glimpse of heaven.

Although many of those who have had a near-death experience will struggle to put what they saw into earthly language, descriptions usually try to capture the beauty and the feelings of peace, bliss and contentment. Like the night visions in Chapter Three, many people will emphasize how vivid everything was. They try to describe how there are sights and sounds that aren't like anything they have ever encountered, colours they have never seen, glorious music they have never heard or thought possible. Everything feels so alive, so much so that some people even find it hard to adjust once they come back to earth because it doesn't feel so real by comparison.

One of the earliest modern accounts of an experience that could be described as a near-death experience was in Thomas de Quincey's *Confessions of an English Opium-Eater* in 1821:

> *Having in her childhood fallen into a river ... she saw in a moment her whole life ... arrayed before her as a mirror, not successively, but simultaneously ... there was no pain or conflict ... in a single instant succeeded a dazzling rush of light ...*

It wasn't until much later that Dr Raymond Moody coined the phrase 'near-death experience' in his 1975 book *Life After Life*. At the start of the book, Moody created a description of a near-death experience that included all of the features that he understood to be common to individual accounts:

At the moment a dying man hears the doctor pronounce him dead he begins to hear loud and strange noise and gets the feeling that he is moving fast through a dark and long tunnel. Next he feels himself step outside of his physical body and he can see his body hovering over it from above. He observes the attempt at resuscitation. This is an intensely emotional time but he starts to notice that he still has a 'body' but a different one with different qualities from the one he sees in front of him.

At this point other things begin to take place. Spirits – warm, loving spirits of those who have died – welcome him and help him and a being of light also appears. This being communicates to him without words and asks him to evaluate his life by showing him a panoramic review of key moments in his life.

Next he approaches a barrier that represents the limit between this life and the next. He longs to cross over, intoxicated by feelings of joy, love and peace, but feels he must go back to earth and that it is not yet his time to pass. Somehow he reconnects with his physical body.

When he recovers he tries to explain to others what he experienced but finds that no words are sufficient to describe the world of spirit. His approach to life changes profoundly, most especially his ideas about life and death.

It was Dr Moody who brought near-death experiences into the realms of science, when before they had been confined to either religion or philosophy. Whenever you bring the attention of scientists to a subject, you are going to be opening up a huge debate and loud demands for evidence. It places those people who have actually experienced a near-death or out-of-body experience in a very vulnerable position where others will pull apart every detail, looking for a sign that either they made it up or that there is a perfectly logical explanation for the visions, such as lack of oxygen to the brain. But fortunately, along with the advances in medicine that are bringing increasing numbers of people back from the brink of death or even beyond, society is becoming much more accepting of the stories those people bring back with them. Whether we choose to believe these accounts are proof of the afterlife, as I do, or prefer to think of them as visions within the person's own subconscious, what is not in doubt is that they occur and that they change the lives of those who experience them.

It is also interesting how literature, and nowadays other forms of culture, like film and TV, have included descriptions of near-death experiences. This extract from Emily Brontë's *Wuthering Heights* echoes the research that tells us how many people who go through a near-death experience don't always want to come back.

> *Heaven did not seem to be my home; and I broke my heart with weeping to come back to earth; and the angels were so angry that they flung me out into the middle of the heath on the top of Wuthering Heights; where I woke sobbing for joy.*

Dr Moody identified up to fifteen characteristics of a near-death experience, although he stressed that an individual's account would rarely contain all of these. Over the years that I have been researching and collecting stories in this area myself, I have pinpointed six characteristic sensations that appear to be consistent elements of near-death accounts:

Out-of-body experiences

Often when a person is very close to death, they will find themselves floating up to the ceiling of the hospital room, so that they are looking down on their own body. This is an out-of-body sensation, and although there might be an initial feeling of panic or confusion, this is usually replaced by tangible feelings of complete understanding and peace. Accounts will often describe how a person knows they are no longer in their physical body but they still have a sense of some kind of spiritual body, although they find it hard to describe.

This is what happened to Yvonne, who sent me her story.

My last breath

Some years ago I found out I needed to have a hysterectomy. In the weeks leading up to the operation I started to get a strong feeling that something was going to happen to me. It wasn't just a case of worrying – I'd never had this feeling before previous operations. I tried to put it out of my mind and decided to go ahead with having the operation. Even as I was taken down to the theatre, the surgeon looked at me and said not to be so worried, everything was going to be all right.

The next thing I remember is waking up on the ward and complaining that I felt unwell. The nurse comforted me and told me to go back to sleep. I must have fallen asleep again, but the next thing I remember is the strong feeling of being pulled sideways. I felt myself take the deepest of breaths and then my lungs emptying – it felt like I was taking my last breath. Then, the most peaceful feeling came over my body – waves of love, peace and harmony, no panic or worry. I could see a nurse standing at the end of the bed, with an old-fashioned nurse's hat and navy blue cardigan on. She was smiling at me. I also saw a small man in a cream suit walk past my bed and into the corridor, which was filled with gold light.

Eventually I came round and the patient in the next bed spoke to me: 'God, you had a lucky escape last night. You were surrounded by seven or eight doctors and nurses. You were blue.'

The portal

It is possible to have an out-of-body experience and then return to one's body without reaching this next sensation, which appears to be when people will most often realize that they may be close to death or that they are experiencing something that is related to death in some way, even if they feel confused and unsure exactly what is happening. The portal sensation is when there is a sense of a tunnel or passageway, where typically it is very dark and they find themselves travelling towards a bright and often extremely intense light. For some people, this sensation of travelling may feel like going through space or a black hole, or for others it feels as though they are going up a staircase or, as one person wrote, it was like they were 'swimming' up a hillside through the long grass.

For Gwen, it was the feeling that she was being pulled upwards in a whirlwind that transported her through the roof of the hospital in which she was being treated.

My turning point

When I was fourteen years old – this was in 1995 – I be-came seriously ill with a rare auto-immune disease. I'd gone from being an active, sociable fourteen-year-old girl to sud-denly being in intensive care, fighting for my life. As I come from a Catholic family, I was given the last rites during this time.

When I regained consciousness in intensive care, I kept drifting in and out of a heavy sleep. At about 3 a.m. one morning, I could sense someone sitting on the side of my bed and holding my hand. When I asked the nurse who it was, she said it was in the early hours of the morning and no one had been to see me. I was sure it was my angel.

A few days later, my health had stabilized enough for me to be transferred to a High Dependency Unit. I was still very poorly and I had no idea what the future held for me, or whether I was ever going to recover.

My dad had fallen asleep in a chair beside my bed, and I remember looking at the clock in front of me. It was 1 a.m. exactly. Suddenly, I felt a huge surge of joy and power rush into my body. I felt as if I had been engulfed in some kind of whirlwind, and that I could feel myself crashing out of the hospital roof. I had so much energy.

From that moment on, I knew everything was going to be okay. I just knew it. It was a turning point for me. It wasn't my time to die and I had to concentrate on getting better. And I did. I became well enough to go back to school and live a normal life.

I can still 'smell' my angel from time to time – a smell I can only describe as vanilla, but I could never recreate it. I just know that I'm not alone, and that I have to carry on and live life to the best of my abilities.

Thank you for bringing your inspiring books into my life.

Reunions

After the sensation of a tunnel, of going upwards or travelling in some way through time and space, some may find they have already turned back and returned to their physical body, as was the case for Gwen. But for others, they will typically find themselves bathed in light, in an incredibly beautiful, magical, heavenly place. Here they will be greeted by one or a number of spiritual beings, usually loved ones who have already departed, but not always someone they know or recognize.

Elaine told me the story of her mother, who returned from her near-death experience with visions of the most beautiful garden.

The golden gate

When I was a child my mother had a very bad motorbike accident. She told me that she had a near-death experience when she was in hospital and they thought she had died. She said she went through a passageway and came out into a beautiful garden where she saw a golden gate. On the other side of the gate was her grandma, who told her she couldn't come through but had to go back, so she eventually found herself back in the hospital, where she stayed for some months.

For Owen, the message during his near-death experience when he found himself suddenly in heaven was clear: it wasn't his time yet.

I've been to heaven

The year was 1945 and I was five years old, lying in a make-shift tent over my bed. A steam kettle with Friars' Balsam was helping me to breathe but the doctor's prognosis was very poor. I had double pneumonia with pleurisy and was not expected to live, so my mother and grandmother took turns to sit with me during the night.

You know how when you are child in a pushchair and you fall asleep, you suddenly wake up in Woolworths and have no idea how you got there? Well, I woke up on a hillside. I now liken it to a Swiss Alpine meadow, but even more beautiful. There were so many different types and colours of flowers growing through the grass, white-blossomed trees and in the distance mauve-coloured mountains. I had never seen mountains before.

I knew where I was and said to myself, 'This is heaven.' I felt so alive and content. I was suddenly aware of a man approaching. He wore a white robe but was an average-looking guy. His brown eyes looked sternly at me. He spoke to me with a rich and strong voice: 'You are not ready yet. You must go back.'

Suddenly I was winging my way through a black void following a silvery-blue shining cord that seemed attached somewhere to my body. I felt no fear, and then I was squeezed back into my body – I had to scrunch up to fit into it! I awoke and said to my grandmother, 'Nanny, I've been to heaven and it was wonderful but a man told me I was not ready yet and sent me back.' She stroked my head and smiled. The experience has flavoured my life. I think he must be my spirit guide.

Ana Rita had a frightening brush with near-death while in an elevator. She didn't suffer any lasting harm, but appreciates her celestial helpers turning up when they did to jolt her into consciousness.

Just going for a bike ride

I've been wanting to write to you. I've just discovered one of your books ... well, I bought it in January and started just this week. I wanted to read it but at the same time until recently I was a little unsure but since I got the courage to start, now I can't stop.

I'm thirty years old and have a degree in psychology. I've always felt a bit different but I'm still kind of afraid of what can come next. I'm not sure when I started to see or feel 'something' but I do remember some specific moments. I'm very curious about these issues and I would like to open myself to them more, except that where I live it isn't really accepted.

Let me tell you about something that happened to me when I was fourteen years old. I was going to go for a bike ride with my mom. We lived on the eleventh floor of our building so we had to take the elevator, one of us in each of the building's two elevators as they were small and we had our bikes. My mother went first and then my elevator got there almost at the same time.

Usually I would put the bike in first and then I would enter. But that day I went for a shortcut and just got in backwards with the wheels facing the door. The door shut and I pressed the button, and then everything happened so fast. When the elevator started going down the bike was rolling up and my neck was under the handlebar. I started to choke and couldn't get out from under the bar. It was really pressing into my neck and I was completely stuck. I just remember throwing my arm out in the direction of the buttons, but I couldn't even see them. At that moment I fainted and I was literally hanging by the throat. I could hear myself struggling to breathe, and then in the next second I was suddenly in the hall of our apartment with the door in front of me. I could still hear myself struggling to breathe. Between me and the door there was a someone who looked like a very, very tall person, except that in the place of their head there was just light, incredibly bright light. The person or being talked to me and said, 'Rita, stop playing, this is very serious, stop playing! Wake up!' It gave me comfort, strength, warmth, and then my eyes opened! I was still hanging by the neck in the elevator and I was having a lot of trouble breathing but I stood up and, somehow, pushed the bike away and got free. This only happened in seconds but it felt like hours.

The elevator had stopped between the eighth and the ninth floor. I put the bike in a corner, away from me, pushed the button and started going down. My mother had seen the elevator when it stopped and she didn't know what was happening. She opened the door and my neck was red, of course. I told her what happened and she believed me but we never really talked about it so I am glad to write to you now.

Life review

We are all familiar nowadays with the phrase 'my life flashed before my eyes', and this is certainly a common sensation described in accounts of near-death experiences. It is fascinating that researchers studying this area have discovered that as technology has changed the ways in which we view images, so have the ways in which people see their every moment flash before them changed, with reports now of panoramic images like a 360-degree 3D movie screen. What is even more fascinating to me is that this is the sensation that offers those who go through this experience the opportunity not just to see their whole life before their eyes, but to understand all the consequences of their actions, both positive and negative.

And the message that every single person brings back from this experience? It is that love is all that matters. Remember Gwen's story from a few pages back. As a child she had been taken very ill with an auto-immune disease and described how she felt she was rising up through the hospital roof and also was visited by a spirit in her hospital bed. Gwen wrote to me again to let me know about the message she given to bring back with her, one of love, even in the face of death.

Don't be afraid

I remember when I was very poorly, before being taken into intensive care, I knew that I was dying. I wasn't scared, but I felt sad for the people I was leaving behind (my mum and dad were so devastated they could barely be in the same room as me). I couldn't take their pain away, although I was perfectly accepting of my own impending death.

At the same time, when I was drifting in and out of consciousness, I remember I saw a huge great big circle of yellow light. There were all sorts of people walking towards and past me – people walking their dogs, people in suits going to work, children and their mums – but I was walking 'against the grain' and returned to my body.

At the end of all this, I carried a message with me throughout life, and that was, 'Never be afraid of death.' I no longer remember who told me this, or why I carry it with me, but it does certainly offer me some peace. That was nearly twenty years ago now.

When I first read your book a few weeks ago, I was talking to my husband about what I had read about the angels, and my own experiences, when suddenly a vase of roses on our kitchen table moved across the table. It was very peaceful, and so special. I feel more surrounded by angels now than ever before. I am so grateful to your books for opening my eyes to life and what's really important.

Eternity

It is often the case that those who have had a near-death experience get to a place where the usual earthly barriers of time and place are dissolved. Suddenly it feels as though they are in three places at once, or they might travel forward or backwards in time – eternity literally opens up before them. It may sound like the stuff of science fiction, but it's quite amazing how some people have literally been able to recount things that have happened while they were in a coma and apparently completely cut off from the world.

This was the case for the famous psychiatrist Carl Jung. Jung recounted his own incredible near-death experience in his autobiography, *Memories, Dreams and Reflections*.

The most glorious thing I had ever seen

It seemed to me that I was high up in space. Far below I saw the globe of the earth, bathed in a gloriously blue light. I saw the deep blue sea and the continents. Far below my feet lay Ceylon, and in the distance ahead of me the subcontinent of India. My field of vision did not include the whole earth, but its global shape was plainly distinguishable and its outlines shone with a silvery gleam through that wonderful blue light. In many places the globe seemed coloured, or spotted dark green like oxidized silver. Far away to the left lay a broad expanse – the reddish-yellow desert of Arabia; it was as though the silver of the earth had there assumed a reddish-gold hue.

Then came the Red Sea, and far, far back – as if in the upper left of a map – I could just make out a bit of the Mediterranean. My gaze was directed chiefly towards that. Everything else appeared indistinct. I could also see the snow-covered Himalayas, but in that direction it was foggy or cloudy. I did not look to the right at all. I knew that I was on the point of departing from the earth. Later I discovered how high in space one would have to be to have so extensive a view – approximately a thousand miles! The sight of the earth from this height was the most glorious thing I had ever seen.

Jung felt a sense of profound disappointment when he was 'shocked' back into life – it was such an 'unspeakably glorious' vision to him that he said it took a good three weeks before he was able to truly make up his mind to live again. As Eben Alexander wrote in his book *Proof of Heaven: A Neurosurgeon's Journey into the Afterlife*, 'Our eternal spiritual self is more real than anything we perceive in this physical realm.'

Lawrence wrote to me to share his near-death experience. All five sensations are present in his vivid account.

Did I want to go through?

I had a near-death experience in 1973. I had a bad reaction to a medication at the dentist's surgery and ended up having a heart attack. I came out of my body, saw myself dead on the floor and was taken through a tunnel by a ghostly white car towards a bright light.

When I reached the end of the tunnel I saw and was greeted by a young lady and a boy of about eighteen years of age. I couldn't look at them face on because of the incredible light they gave off, so I squinted at them and looked as best I could. They welcomed me, speaking in my mind through telepathy, and asked me if I wanted to enter the garden ahead, which was a beautiful scene of flowers, trees, greens and river streams. I saw glass and marble mansion-type buildings ahead and was in awe at the sight. I felt so elated and happy, I wanted to stay there and not move. Suddenly I was lifted up eighteen inches or so from the floor so that I could see even further and I saw people, and animals running about – they all had solid bodies and were very real. I knew where I was but didn't care as I was filled with love and peace.

I then saw a cinema screen appear in my mind, which then became a huge screen ahead of me. It showed me myself from the age of five to old age – everything was going at a tremendous speed. At this time a voice asked if I wanted to enter and I replied that I might do, but my reply sounded almost like a question. On the screen I then saw images from all around the world; I saw wars and a tsunami submerging a country into an Atlantis-type state. But then I also saw good things like medical cures being found.

Suddenly I began to come back to the ground and I walked towards a gate. There, two light beings or angels asked me if I wanted to go through, because if I did then I couldn't go back to Earth's realm. I half-entered the gate and at the moment I began to enter, I felt eighteen again. A blue-violet light came towards me and I was mesmerized; I felt the light feeding me with knowledge directly into my mind, teaching me about the Universe.

I didn't go through the gate but returned, although I feel

like I have been given an amazing gift. It appears that even my heart was repaired in the afterlife and when I recently had an angiogram the doctors were amazed at how good my arteries are now at sixty-two years of age. I've even been able to predict some of the future as I seem to remember something new every day, but I won't go into that in this letter!

I wish I could devote a whole book to near-death experiences as they are, in my opinion, perhaps the best proof we have that the afterlife is real, but sadly there isn't time to discuss more here. If you do want learn more, may I recommend Raymond Moody's classic book *Life after Life: Survival of Bodily Death* as well as *On Death and Dying* by Elisabeth Kübler-Ross and, of course, my own book *The Afterlife Is Real*.

You may also want to visit IANDS, the International Association for Near-Death Studies: http://iands.org/home.html IANDS is one of the longest-standing and most important near-death organizations, with a wealth of fascinating material for you to discover and to inspire you. Paul's story, below, is published on their website and I couldn't think of a better way to round off this section than with his incredible and uplifting story.

Paul's Story

My friend and his girlfriend stayed with me while we waited for the ambulance. They also came to the hospital with me. I was bleeding heavily from a potentially fatal injury. In the emergency room, I saw a South African doctor. In the middle of his examination, he was called away to an emergency chest operation to save someone's life. While he was away, I remember I was talking to my friend's girlfriend when I lost consciousness.

It was such a relaxed feeling, just slipping away like that. My whole being seemed to change. The first thing I noticed was an amazing sense of relaxation and calm. I noticed that every single negative human emotion had simply gone, which left me feeling absolutely wonderful. Imagine the biggest high of your life, multiply it by a thousand, and you still won't even be close to this wonderful, safe feeling.

Then I found myself in a blue tunnel. The colour was an electric blue, similar to the kind you get on certain L.E.D. Christmas lights now. It was a very vivid and wonderful colour. I floated gently, quite slowly along this tunnel and fully relaxed. I can even give you the dimensions of the tunnel. It was 2000 feet in diameter. Eventually, I could see in the distance a point that was a hive of tremendous activity. At this point, the blue tunnel turned into the white tunnel, a very clear line of transition. It was impossible to see into the white tunnel, as there was so much light pouring out from it. There was also a tremendous feeling of love emanating from this source, and a kind of instant knowledge. You just knew it. The blue tunnel could accommodate two-way traffic, whereas the white tunnel was one-way for souls leaving the earth plane. Once you crossed over into the white tunnel there was no going back.

The light from this tunnel was so bright that under normal circumstances it would have been blinding, but here it was warm, safe and full of love. As I got closer to the transition point between the blue and white tunnels, the activity became clearer. I could clearly see many, many souls on both sides of the transition point. There were quite a few souls, like myself, coming from the earth plane. All of these souls were being met by groups of souls who had come from the white tunnel. It was like each soul had its own entourage of souls from the other side to meet them. Some were being welcomed with open arms and carefully guided through the transition point and into the wonderful light of the white tunnel; some were being greeted with discussions; and some were being turned back towards the earth plane.

When I finally reached the transition, the first thing I did was carefully look around. This is how I gained my knowledge about the diameter of the tunnel. It was quite an amazing sight to behold, this transition point, with all the many souls coming and going. It was a very busy place, and most unexpected! When I was met by my own entourage of souls, I could clearly see that they were human, but in this existence were beings of light. They seemed to be the same colour as the electric blue in the first tunnel. I was greeted with a great love and urgency. I was held, and knowledge was imparted to me. I was told this was not my time, but that this was meant to happen. It was the only way my life could change onto the right path. I was given so much knowledge that it would overflow in your head normally, but I was told that each piece of knowledge would become available to me when needed. The knowledge that was given to me at that moment, which I felt to the core of my being, was this: Time is just an illusion created by humanity; it simply

Theresa Cheung

does not exist. From the other side you can travel to any period in time as easily as crossing the street.

It is hard to describe the feeling of home that these souls brought with them. I knew them all, but am unsure how as my time there was limited. Eventually, I had to say goodbye and was returned to my body so fast that I awoke with a start, which shocked the faces of the South African doctor and my friends. Apparently, when I lost consciousness, I had lost so much blood that my heart stopped beating. My friends found the doctor, who took one look at me and punched me really hard in the ribcage above my heart. This brought me straight back. This doctor later told me he had worked in war zones in Africa, so was used to working on people with very little equipment. This was fortunate for me, having been still in the emergency-room waiting area! For some reason, the first thing I checked when I came back was that my ring finger was okay. I watched with a deep fascination as the doctor put my wrist back together. He had to reach right up inside my arm to retrieve a snapped tendon, which he sewed back together. All I could think of at this point was the film *Terminator 2* when he takes the skin off his hand to show he is a robot!

Eventually I regained most of the use of my hand. I can still only feel properly in half of it, as the other half was completely numb for years. Some nerves have now grown back jumbled. For example, if I touch the base of my thumb, I feel it in my index finger. But, I learn to live with it and still manage to type and play keyboard, despite only having full use of seven out of my ten digits.

I was told that I was clinically dead for at least thirty seconds, which doesn't sound very long. Yet it was plenty of time to experience my NDE, which seemed like hours to me at the time. It took me a long time to recover mentally as I went through a lot. As a result, I lost my job and then two months later I came home on my twenty-fifth birthday to find my flatmate had put a padlock on the outside of my door. He told me, 'You don't live here anymore.' It was clear that he was just after my flat and went to any lengths to get it.

So I lost my job, found myself homeless, and was distraught. Years later, I can now appreciate the whole experience. The path I was on, I would probably have worked myself to death. Currently I am thirty-nine years old and just about to start my own astrology business, but it has taken years and years of soul-searching to get to where I am now. I am even more of a spiritual person than I was, with an unbreakably strong belief in reincarnation and karma. The main difference now is that I have proof of my own beliefs and of the life on the other side as being our true home. I have no fear of death. Death is not the end, only a transition to our true home.

I have always felt very uneasy about death, even fearful of it. This is despite my family being full of members who have been able to be in touch with the afterlife; I've always been convinced there is more than just this one physical life but my belief that death is really just another beginning hasn't always managed to allay my personal anxieties about my mortality. I've had some mind-blowing and life-changing experiences which have convinced me absolutely at the time that death is not the end – experiences

Theresa Cheung

which have given me an absolute conviction that heaven is close by – but being the flawed human being I am I always seem to need more and more reassurance. One experience is never enough and as the days, weeks, months, years go by, I start second-guessing myself, questioning whether it was all coincidence or imagination or wish-fulfilment and that is why reading the stories sent to me from people all over the world is so uplifting and energizing. Perhaps it is a fear of the unknown, or a fear that I won't have made the most of my time here on earth, but I am able to draw great comfort, conviction and hope from the stories I read from those who have crossed over, come back and been generous enough to tell the tale. All of us cannot be wrong! There is more to this life than meets the eye.

Death is one of the last taboos, especially in Western cultures. We tend not to talk very openly about it, preferring to keep it tucked away in some cupboard somewhere where it has the habit of turning into a monster in our subconscious. I think this is why I admire the work of Elisabeth Kübler-Ross, who wrote books including *On Death and Dying*, in which she explored what she thought to be the five stages of facing death: denial, anger, bargaining, depression and acceptance. After the death of my mother I made things incredibly difficult for myself by going to extremes in the denial stage. I didn't want anything to do with my mother. Just looking at her spectacle case or the last book she read with the marker still in it felt like a dagger to my heart, so I gathered all her possessions together and threw them away, only keeping a small shoe box which I stored under my bed. It was as if removing all memories and not thinking or talking about my mother would somehow make the pain go away, but, of course, it didn't and in time the memories refused to be contained and flooded back, threatening to drown me with feelings of anger which eventually subsided into a deep depression. If, however, I had been more spiritually prepared during and after her death I think my grief journey would have been less traumatic and drawn out. I made things harder for myself by trying to deny the existence of heaven and the very real possibility that my mother wasn't gone forever but was with me eternally in spirit.

Brain scientist and stroke survivor Jill Bolte Taylor wrote in her recent memoir, *My Stroke of Insight*, her own observations of her near-death experience:

> *My perception of my physical boundaries was no longer limited to where skin met air. I felt like a genie liberated from his bottle . . . My entire self-concept shifted as I no longer perceived myself as a single, a solid, an entity with boundaries that separated me from the entities around me. I understood that at the most elementary level, I am a fluid.*

Taylor's book is a great step towards building better bridges between science and the humanities – because if we can make connections between medical and spiritual care then we are more likely to make improvements in both care for the terminally ill, in terms of preparing for a good death, and care for those left behind, in how we are better able come to terms with our grief and our own feelings about life and death, and beyond.

Final word

When we finally know we are dying, and all other sentient beings are dying with us, we start to have a burning, almost heartbreaking sense of the fragility and preciousness of each moment and each being, and from this can grow a deep, clear, limitless compassion for all beings.

Sogyal Rinpoche, *The Tibetan Book of Living and Dying*

I hope that the stories in this book have gone some way to show that the conversations we can have with heaven are indeed a two-way experience. When we are having a really good conversation we are completely attentive; we listen and speak, we learn from each other, we offer things like comfort or encouragement, sometimes we laugh and sometimes we share each other's tears. Whether we are having a chat with a friend or a conversation with heaven, these things are still true.

I think the best thing about being touch with heaven is that the only language we need to use is one of love. It is love that infuses every divine moment or sign, and all these moments remind us both that we are never alone and that life here on earth is truly precious. Moments of connection remind us of compassion and kindness. And I think something that is shared by all the stories collected in these pages is a sense of one's attention being caught. Sometimes we need a tap on the shoulder or a visit from an old, departed soul to remind us of all the love that is right in front of us in our own lives.

For me, developing a connection with the afterlife has been of incredible help during my experiences of depression. Just when I have needed it most, support has come to me in any number of mysterious ways; a visit from my mum in a dream, the kindness of a stranger on a bench. This connection has saved me from the depths of despair, but perhaps even more magically, it is the small moments of wonder that now speak to me: the sudden appearance of a bright white feather, or a happy coincidence. Over the years, my confidence in my intuition, or my inner spiritual guide, has grown. I've also found the courage to ask for help when I've needed it, a lesson which I believe comes through very loud and clear in many of the stories here.

As humans we tend to think of conversations as purely spoken words, but I hope you will have seen in these chapters just how many other ways there are in which it is possible to connect and communicate: through touch, sounds, beauty, nature, energy and more. And as you develop your powers of attention more, I hope you will find that the human connections in your life deepen at the same time. Just as we nourish our relationship with the afterlife, we nourish our relationship with this life.

> *Earth's crammed with heaven . . .*
> *But only he who sees takes off his shoes.*
> Elizabeth Barrett Browning

Sometimes we have to allow ourselves to pause and reflect so that we might be more attentive to the details of our life and what is going on around us. Sometimes we need to get out into the world and take off our shoes, knowing that we are supported both here in this life and beyond. If we are still for long enough then a butterfly may come to rest on our shoulder; if we allow peace to fill our hearts then we will be able to share the precious gift of peace with others. Because just as we communicate with words, we also connect through our emotions and energy. Once we understand that there is no limit when it comes to love, we can truly receive it into our hearts and become the most generous and loving person we can be.

As we have seen in many of the stories, entering into a conversation with heaven can be very comforting in times of grief or pain. It is always important to understand that having a direct connection with heaven does not necessarily mean all your troubles will go away. The spiritual guides can offer guidance and support, and help us to access our own insight and intuition, but they are not there simply to cure all of our ills. If that were the case, there would be no reason for people to ever endure hardships or pain. This is a difficult idea to swallow at times, to try and explain why bad things happen to good people. I'm not sure we will ever completely understand, especially during our time here on earth, but I do believe that testing times can lead to spiritual growth by acting as a catalyst for positive change.

Above all else, my hope is that these stories show that in addition to offering a hand of support in times of grief or mental anguish, connecting with heaven doesn't have to happen only when you're close to death – you don't need that shock – and that you can be open to receiving inspirational thoughts and advice about living in spirit on a daily basis.

Remember that spiritual beings are always with you, but you need to meet them halfway and enter into the conversation yourself. Don't be afraid to speak to them, and always remember to listen. I find that spending just a little time in quiet contemplation each day is extremely beneficial in not only developing my spiritual connection but also in nurturing feelings of calm and peace, even my creativity and sense of purpose.

It is by living each day with meaning and purpose and with a loving heart that you do your part in bringing heaven closer to earth. And the more people who do that, the easier it is for us all to talk to heaven.

You may wonder how I know for sure that each one of us can connect to the other side. I don't know . . . I believe. There have been moments of serious doubt and crisis along the way but I have never truly lost my belief. I'm not asking you to agree with me – or even to believe – all I'm asking you to do now you have read this book is to open your mind to the very real possibility that heaven exists and communication between this world and the next is not a fantasy but a reality. Open your mind to that wonderful possibility and you may just find that your life transforms in magical ways.

> *What if you slept? And what if, in your sleep, you dreamed? And what if, in your dream, you went to heaven and there plucked a beautiful flower? And what if, when you awoke, you had the flower in your hand? Ah, what then?*
>
> Samuel Taylor Coleridge

Calling all spirits

If you have a story or insight you would like to share, or a burning question you need answered or would like to discuss further, don't hesitate to get in touch with me. I welcome after-life and spirit stories, as well as thoughts and questions. If you are at all nervous about getting in touch, I hope it will be a comfort to know that you are not alone, that many other people share similar experiences to your own.

You can write to me care of my publisher:

Simon & Schuster
1st Floor, 222 Gray's Inn Road
London WC1X 8HB

Or email me direct at angeltalk710@aol.com

I would be very happy to hear from you, and with the loving guidance of heaven will try to answer all messages personally, as communicating with you, my readers, is the best thing about writing these books and the reason I write them.

www.theresacheung.com

To wake at dawn with a winged heart, and give thanks
for another day of loving . . .

Kahlil Gibran